# GOD SIGHTINGS

To my friends and family:

In December of 2004, I had a life changing event occur. I found and acknowledge God's saving grace. My friend, Joyce Williams, has included my story in the attached book on page 57. Please read it as it is my prayer for you and yours.

Joyfully,

Wayne

# G

SIGHTINGS

STORIES OF GOD'S
MIRACULOUS PROVISION

# D

JOYCE
WILLIAMS

BEACON HILL PRESS
OF KANSAS CITY

ISBN 978-0-8341-2470-7

Printed in the
United States of America

Cover Design: Brandon Hill
Interior Design: Sharon Page

**Library of Congress Cataloging-in-Publication Data**

God sightings : stories of God's miraculous provision / compiled by Joyce Williams.
   p. cm.
  ISBN 978-0-8341-2470-7 (pbk.)
  1. Miracles—Anecdotes. I. Williams, Joyce, 1944-
  BT97.3.G64 2009
  231.7'30922—dc22

2009024958

10 9 8 7 6 5 4 3 2 1

# CONTENTS

*The fruit of silence is prayer.*
*The fruit of prayer is faith.*
*The fruit of faith is love.*
*The fruit of love is service.*
*The fruit of service is peace.*

*—Mother Teresa*

———•———

# ACKNOWLEDGMENTS

It is awesome to be reminded that our God still performs miracles today. Working with these contributors from around the world and hearing stories of glimpses of God through His miraculous provision have blessed my heart tremendously. I've praised God as I've delighted in each contributor's account of God's divine intervention.

I express my deepest appreciation to everyone who has participated in this book. May the precious divine miracle-worker continue to bless each of you with His continued provision as He intersects your path. And may your life be filled with God sightings for all your days.

# FOREWORD

Quite frankly, I wasn't expecting a miracle when in 2005 I crossed paths with Joyce Williams in Branson, Missouri. We were both presenting at a weeklong Christian women's gathering. I arrived earlier to deliver a keynote address, and she came later in the week to facilitate a workshop. I attended the workshop, expressed my appreciation, and we immediately bonded. For women that means shopping—buying matching outfits at Dressin' Gaudy—lunching, talking, talking, and talking.

Laughing, we realized we were "twins," born in the same month of the same year but separated for decades. Yes, Joyce and I refer to each other as twin. We call each other our *only* twin. Even my family and friends refer to her as my twin. I'm not sure they even know her name.

My twin has entitled this book *God Sightings*. I like to refer to those miraculous moments as supernatural intrusions: *supernatural* because only a sovereign God could arrange the miracle; *intrusions* because they don't always feel gentle, but since they're from God they're always good.

As you read this book, you'll journey with men and women of different ages who are in different stages of life as they share miracles—expected *and unexpected*—that have affected their lives. Rejoice with them as you hear of God's grace, love, and mercy in each page of this inspirational book.

The verse I've chosen to give my twin as a gift for all the hard work that goes into compiling a book is "He [she] who refreshes others will himself [herself] be refreshed" (Proverbs 11:25).

Thank you, dear twin, for refreshing so many in so many ways and for sharing this book. May we all have the spiritual wisdom that trickles from deep places in our hearts to recognize those miracles that come into our lives, unpredictably but often, because God is good—all the time.

—Rachael Crabb
Author

# A CHANGE OF HEART

## JOYCE WILLIAMS

*I will give you a new heart and put a new spirit in you.*
—Ezekiel 36:26

I'm told on good authority that my baby sister, Jane, and I were first-class brats. We're only fifteen months apart in age. As young children growing up in Roanoke, Virginia, we found it only natural to connive and scheme together in our ongoing search for mischief. With typical motherly love, Mama told us in later years that she couldn't remember how naughty we had been. But a number of witnesses have been more than glad to share their memories with us. We were two ornery girls!

Some Sunday evenings when Daddy and Mama were too sick to attend service, Jane and I enjoyed walking a few blocks to Uncle Lewis's and Aunt Hallie's little Fallon Park Wesleyan Church. Because of our mischievous reputations, we were surprised that they asked us to sing on some of those occasions. Sometimes we got tickled and couldn't finish our "special music" selections. Yet they continued to ask us to sing! I guess it was the "cute little kids" factor at work.

Daddy, Mama, and our older sister, Bobbi, gave their hearts to the Lord a couple of years before I was born. Thus, Jane and I experienced a Christian home and family our entire growing-up years. We were truly blessed.

In the fall of 1951, Mama became critically ill with severe anemia and was hospitalized for almost two weeks. She received several blood transfusions, and when she came home she had lost a lot of weight and was very pale and weak.

Daddy had tried to keep up with his job working for the railroad as a night watchman. Then, a few weeks after Mama came home,

Daddy suffered a heart attack. Suddenly our days and nights were filled with uncertainty. Life became very serious. Bobbi was married with four small children of her own, so I was suddenly in charge—a huge challenge for a third-grader.

I learned to cook. I should rather say I learned to open cans and heat the contents in a pot. I did learn to peel potatoes and usually got them to the table without ruining them. We were so blessed when First Church of the Nazarene, our home church, had a "pounding" for our family and brought over bags of food. I remember how excited Jane and I were as we opened each bag. It was like Christmas in October!

Mama and Daddy were both very weak, and Daddy's doctor told him his prognosis was not good. His heart, weakened from years of smoking prior to becoming a Christian, had been severely damaged. The future for our family seemed grim. *What were we going to do?*

Then something very extraordinary happened. Our pastor, C. William Ellwanger, came calling. Jane and I brought him cookies and a glass of iced tea, which he bravely ate and drank. He sat in our living room and encouraged all four of us and read some scripture.

Then he said, "Brother and Sister Bain, do you believe the Lord can touch both of you?" Mama nodded, and Daddy said, "Oh, I know He's a great miracle-worker. Yes, I believe He can!"

Then Pastor Ellwanger had us gather 'round. He laid his hands on Daddy's shoulders and prayed for him, asking for the Great Physician's touch. Daddy told us later that he felt a sensation like a tiny bolt of lightning tingle through his body. Suddenly he felt much stronger. Then our pastor put his hand on Mama's shoulder and prayed for her. We felt such a sense of God's presence in that room. Daddy and Mama wiped their tears as they walked our pastor to the door.

Daddy went for a follow-up visit the next day. The doctor pulled out his stethoscope and moved it around, listening intently. Then he listened to Daddy's back. Puzzled, he said, "I don't understand this. Your heartbeat is good, and the rhythm is normal." Once again, tears filled Daddy's eyes as he shared what had happened with our crusty old family physician. The doctor sat there amazed. Then he exclaimed, "I believe we have a miracle! Your heart was severely damaged. Now it is sounds quite normal."

As Daddy slipped on his shirt and headed out the door, he whispered over and over, "Praise the Lord!" And we rejoiced together around the dinner table that evening as we ate Mama's good home cooking once again.

That fall of 1951 changed our family—especially Jane and me. We were no longer the "mischievous Bain girls." Oh, we weren't perfect, but it's true that no one is ever quite the same after witnessing the touch of the Great Physician.

The next time we sang in church, Jane and I didn't get the giggles. We held hands, joyfully singing our thanksgiving. We had reason to praise the Lord!

Daddy's heart wasn't the only one that had been changed.

PRAYER: *Father, thank you for giving me a change of heart.*

THOUGHT FOR THE DAY: It is the heart that experiences God (Blaise Pascal).

# MY CROSS SCAR

## JUDY ANDERSON

*Remember, O Lord, your great mercy and love.*
—Psalm 25:6

From out of nowhere—*thud!*—followed by the most excruciating pain I've ever experienced. Immediately I heard my son, Ray, who was right there on the lake bank beside me, cry out, "Oh, no! Mother!"

I remember hooking what appeared to be a big rainbow trout and trying to get it to shore. All the others who had been fishing with us had gone on back to the main lodge. Just the three of us die-hards, Ray, Daryl, and I, had stayed behind to toss one more cast while we waited for the dinner bell to clang.

Our family had arrived at Waunita Hot Springs Ranch in Colorado about two hours earlier that Sunday afternoon in June 2000. After attending church that morning in Canon City, Colorado, we had enjoyed lunch and had then driven caravan-style over Monarch Pass down into the Gunnison Valley. We could hardly wait to get started on a fun-filled week. No one looked forward to these times more than Grandpa Daryl and I.

Then came that sudden spine-chilling and indescribable moment. I seemed to fall backward into Ray's arms and heard him cry out, "Oh, no! No!" Incredibly, I was able to make some sense of what had happened. Daryl had moved our vehicle closer and opened the back end to get more fishing gear. When he heard me squeal, he realized I had hooked a fish. So he knew I would need the new needle-nosed pliers I had recently bought. Thinking he was helping, he tossed them to me.

Suddenly those pliers were *in my face.* I felt as if my nose or my face had cracked wide open. I shrieked when Ray pulled them from the side of my nose. I heard Daryl scream, "Oh, Judy! Oh, no! What have

I done?" My face was covered with blood that streamed into my eyes and down my neck, blinding and choking me. I couldn't breathe.

Lying there flat on the ground, I felt as if my life were fading away. I was consumed with prayers I wanted answered—especially the salvation of precious loved ones. I had to know they had accepted Jesus as their Lord and Savior!

Then someone yelled, "Get her into a sitting position—she's strangling on her own blood!" I remember ice being put on my face as Daryl helped keep me sitting upright and then got me into the back of our truck. Ray drove, comforting us by singing at the top of his voice as we raced to the hospital in Gunnison.

Miraculously, I remained conscious and without fear. I clearly recall begging Daryl and Ray, "Promise me you'll make sure they're all saved!"

The emergency room staff tried to make sense of what had happened to me. After taking X-rays, the doctor sewed up my face and lip and kept assuring me that I had experienced a miracle. If the pliers had struck only a few centimeters in either direction, I could easily have been killed or at least blinded. I spent the night in the hospital to be sure my blood pressure was stabilized. It had been very high immediately following the accident.

I recovered slowly. For weeks my front teeth, gums, upper lip, and side of my nose were very sore. But every time I looked in the mirror I thanked God that I was still alive and could see.

In God's incredible timing, just days before the accident, I had written a heart-felt letter to my family that began with "If today were the last day of my life . . ." Before the accident I always assumed I would have another tomorrow. But I learned that a split second can mean the difference between life and death.

As I recovered, I realized that the worst pain I could ever comprehend would be if I had died without telling my family about Jesus' love. I wanted them to be absolutely certain that He waits for us to ask Him to forgive our sins and be Lord of our lives.

Incredibly, the scar on my nose healed in the shape of a small cross! It has become a poignant reminder of my very close brush with death. More than ever, I'm keenly aware of just how fragile and tenuous each moment is. My prayer life intensified enormously. Sharing my faith has become a way of life.

Each time I look in the mirror, I'm reminded of the pain our Lord endured on a cross on a lonely hillside and the scars He wears for our sins. I thank Him for my cross-shaped scar that's a tangible reminder of His great love.

PRAYER: *Thank you, Lord, for your gift of everlasting life that was nailed to the Cross for all who believe.*

THOUGHT FOR THE DAY: Our main business is not to see what lies dimly at a distance, but to do what lies clearly at hand (Thomas Carlyle).

# I BELIEVE IN MIRACLES

## LARRY BELEW

*The whole crowd of disciples began joyfully to praise God*
*for all the miracles they had seen.*

—Luke 19:37

In December 1999 my wife, Judie, and I were preparing for a major move from Wichita, Kansas, to The Lamb's Church in Times Square in New York City. We weren't kids just out of college. In fact, we had grown daughters who chided us, "We're supposed to be the ones to grow up and run away from home. Our parents aren't supposed to be doing that!"

But God had made His call clear. In preparation, we sold our home and cars and got rid of everything we couldn't cram into a seventeen-foot U-Haul rental truck. Judie's motto was "Whatever it takes." God led us faithfully at every turn.

The day I accepted the position at The Lamb's, we made two visits. I went to church to tell Gene Williams, our pastor with whom I had served on staff for thirteen years, that we were moving. He took some comfort in my explanation that "God has called us to a new mission field."

Our second visit was to Jonette Anderson, our local missionary organization president. She and her husband, Jess, were veterans of numerous mission trips to The Lamb's. They had recently created one staff apartment and started a second. Pastor John Calhoun at The Lamb's said we could have that apartment, but he wouldn't be able to get a team there to finish it until three months later, in March.

Judie had informed me that if we were moving to New York City, she had to be there by New Year's Eve. She had always wanted to experience the New Year's Eve celebration in Times Square. So with that mandate, we walked into the Anderson home, and I unceremoniously said, "We're moving to New York City in December. Will you get a work team together to go finish our apartment?"

Pastor Calhoun described it as "uninhabitable," and he was right. The neglected, reconfigured rooms, built in 1907, had fallen into disrepair and were a long way from resembling an apartment.

Jonette immediately began putting together a work team. Jess had the vision and building expertise to transform the rooms into a habitable home for us. The day we pulled out, a team of our friends from Wichita flew to New York. By the time we arrived in front of The Lamb's, the Wichita team was already on the fifth floor ripping, cutting, hammering, and plumbing to pull together a beautiful and functional space for us.

It took them a week, but they worked miracles and left us with a wonderful place in which to live and work. Through the obedient willingness of His saints, God had provided a place for us to live.

Although that tiny apartment was provided, there was a lot of work to be done, and there were no funds for a salary. I told Pastor Calhoun a place to live and insurance would be enough if he gave me permission to work part-time off-site. Although I didn't have a job, we agreed on those arrangements.

I had determined—for personal reasons that may have involved pride—that I wouldn't write letters to family and friends asking for support. We would work for our income. However, our friends Dave and Judy Narramore, who had been with us on a previous mission to The Lamb's, came to me, and Dave began describing their plan to raise pledges for our support. They had created incentive mugs with a picture of The Lamb's and our names and address on them.

I protested, but Dave calmly replied, "We're going to write support letters." We marveled each month when checks designated for our support showed up in The Lamb's mail like clockwork. God had removed barrier number two.

The Lord also provided a part-time temporary assignment at the Edison School office on Fifth Avenue. That lasted for several weeks until Pastor Calhoun appointed me as the salaried managing director of the ministry.

When we agreed to move, we weren't sure our apartment would be finished in time or that we would have money for support. God used our Christian friends to perform both miracles. However, there were no funds to rent a U-Haul. So we put those expenses on a credit card. I didn't feel that was financially responsible, but Judie continued to remind me, "Whatever it takes."

A couple of weeks before our departure, Ray Cook called Judie at her office and said, "The pastor our Sunday School class was planning to adopt for Christmas isn't available, so we would like to honor you and Larry this Christmas. Come to our progressive dinner and we'll have some gifts for you."

When I saw Ray at church, my pride was still evident when I said, "This is almost embarrassing. You need to take care of struggling pastors in small churches." Ray grinned and said, "Well, Bud, you're there!" Ray always cuts through the goofy dust to get to reality. So we gratefully accepted.

After a tour of Victorian homes, we ended up at the Cooks' house, where they had their class gift exchange. Then they presented a check to us. It was for almost the exact amount of the U-Haul rental!

God knew what we needed from the beginning of our call to New York. He knew where we would live. He knew where we would work. He knew how to find money for necessities. He even used a change in plans and the faithful members of our church to pay for the move.

So, yes, I believe God works in miraculous ways! I've seen His hand at work in my life.

PRAYER: *Thank you, Father, for your provision for all our needs.*

THOUGHT FOR THE DAY: Be careful for nothing, prayerful for everything, thankful for anything (Dwight L. Moody).

# RIGHTEOUS
# RIGHT HAND

## JANE BERRY

*Do not fear, for I am with you. Do not be dismayed,*
*for I am your God. I will strengthen you and help you;*
*I will hold you up with my righteous right hand.*
—Isaiah 41:10

On Valentine's Day 2005 I was expecting a call from the nurse with the results of an MRI. Instead, the doctor came on the line. "You must not waste time coming to my office. I've made an appointment for you to see a brain surgeon today. You have a brain tumor."

For two years I had battled severe headaches, sinus infections, and extreme weakness. When Danny, my husband, made the decision in May 2004 to retire after thirty years with a large company, I closed my in-home beauty salon business, where I had worked for twenty-five years. We sold our house and purchased a motor home for travel. We enjoyed several motor-home trips.

In January 2005 Danny and I left on a Work and Witness trip with our church to South Africa. While building a church during our three-week stay there, I lost the vision in my left eye. When we arrived home, I immediately saw an eye doctor and was sent for the MRI.

I kept the appointment with the brain surgeon and was given the diagnosis of a benign meningioma tumor that originated in the sinus cavity and wrapped around the optic nerve, carotid artery, spinal fluid, and pituitary gland. The surgeon said he knew of three surgeons in the United States who might take my case; he would not risk the surgery himself. The best and closest surgeon was in Little Rock, Arkansas, at the University of Arkansas Medical Center. Risks included blindness, stroke, spinal fluid leakage, paralysis, and even death.

Before retiring that night I was gripped with fear so great I didn't have the words to express it. I turned to Isaiah 41:10 and read, "Do not fear, for I am with you; do not be dismayed, for I am your God. I will strengthen you and help you; I will uphold you with my righteous right hand." I asked Danny to lay hands on me and pray. As he prayed, I lifted my right hand and felt my Father's hand in mine. Then I fell asleep.

The next morning I called Patsy Lewis, friend, prayer partner, and the wife of one of our former pastors. She was at a retreat in Florida and was assigned to a table during prayer time with Genelle Johnson, Jerelyn Rickie, and Jeannie McCullough, all of whom were wives of former pastors of ours, and they prayed for me. Praise the Lord!

Twenty-five people from Oklahoma, Louisiana, Texas, Kentucky, and Arkansas gathered on March 16, 2005, to keep vigil at the hospital during my all-day surgery. I came out of surgery with full vision in both eyes, and the entire tumor had been removed.

Two months later we returned to Oklahoma. My forehead had been removed for a short time during the surgery to get to the tumor, leaving me with nerve damage and terrible headaches. Dr. Kim said I would always be on pain medication and that the damage was permanent.

In April 2006 we began a revival with evangelist Elaine Pettit. Danny insisted I go forward during one of the services to be anointed for healing. I was first in line for Rev. Pettit to lay hands on me, and she prayed silently.

The next day I visited Dr. Kim and asked him to taper me off the drugs. The medication had not stopped the pain and only made me want to stay in bed all the time. I was afraid that if I told Dr. Kim the headaches had stopped after prayer, he would credit the drugs and not God. He agreed, because he knew nothing could change my situation as far as the medical profession was concerned.

After many weeks of decreasing the drugs, I made my last visit to Dr. Kim. While getting ready to go for my appointment, I felt the Holy Spirit dealing with me to share my healing with him.

After my examination, as Dr. Kim was about to leave the room, I blurted out the question "Are you a Christian?"

"Yes, I am."

"Do you believe in divine healing?"

"Yes!" Then Dr. Kim agreed with me that God's divine touch could be the only explanation.

On my last visit to Little Rock, Dr. Al Mefty released me from future visits three years early. He called me his "success story."

On our way home, we decided to sell the motor home. We bought a house five minutes from my old salon, and I went back to work. All my clients came back.

My best friend, Bobbye McElrath, wrote a song for me after hearing my life-changing news. I have her permission to share the lyrics with you:

### He Holds Your Hand

*He'll hold your hand.*
*He'll be with you.*
*Whatever the task,*
*He'll be with you.*
*For this moment He created you*
*To see what He alone can do in you.*
*He'll see you through;*
*He'll heal you too.*
*He holds your hand.*

PRAYER: *Heavenly Father, may I always remember that your hand is extended. Remind me to hold on!*

THOUGHT FOR THE DAY: God is working out all the details. All we have to do is wait for Him and watch with anticipation.

# HIS WORDS
# IN MY MOUTH

## JILL BRISCOE

*"Ah, Sovereign* LORD," *I said, "I do not know how to speak; I am only a child." But the* LORD *said to me, "Do not say 'I am only a child.' You must go to everyone I send you to and say whatever I command you. Do not be afraid of them, for I am with you and will rescue you," declares the* LORD.
—Jeremiah 1:6-8

I'll never forget where I was when I learned about the tragedy of 9/11. Stuart and I had spent six weeks training and traveling throughout Russia. Stuart dropped me off at Heathrow in London. He was headed to northern Ireland, and I was looking forward to going home. I ate dinner and then sat back and relaxed, snoozing happily.

We had been on the plane for about three and a half hours when the pilot came on the intercom. He said, "There's an emergency. All air space and borders are closed. We're making an emergency landing. I can't tell you what it's all about until we're on the ground."

I looked at my watch and wondered, *Where is he landing three and a half hours over the ocean?* Then I grabbed the map and thought, *Oh, Newfoundland.* That's all there was. And sure enough—down we came.

Stuart and I had been training Russian leaders and pastors and conducting missionary meetings and conventions. We had been teaching them how to establish a presence, gain credibility, and speak Christ into their situations.

Suddenly as we descended in the airplane, Psalm 139:16 popped into my mind: "All the days ordained for me were written in your book." I thought, *All the days, Lord—even September 11?* I was reassured. I had not put myself into this situation. God had done it.

So I had established a presence—or God had established it for me. Now it was my turn to take the next step that we had been teaching for six weeks—gain credibility. Then, third, I hoped I could speak Christ into the situation. A huge sense of excitement began inside me as I buckled myself into the will of God for me on September 11, 2001.

A young doctor was sitting next to me. We looked at each other, and I said, "What do you think?"

He replied, "What could have shut all the borders? Perhaps there's a nuclear meltdown somewhere."

I said, "Taliban."

"Taliban?"

"Well," I said, "I've just been in Russia, and they're in the paper every day."

"What can terrorism have to do with America?" he asked.

We continued to bat our theories back and forth until we landed.

Finally we were told what had happened. We sat on the ground for twelve hours before they took us to a little place called Gander, Newfoundland, where we stayed in a Salvation Army hall, living in the pews and on the floor for one of the most God-shadowed weeks of my life. I'm not the same woman.

In times like that you discover all kinds of things you never knew about God. You learn all sorts of things you never knew about yourself, and you find out all sorts of things you never knew about other people. What a joy it was to speak Christ into that situation!

I could have said, "I'm too tired—I'm too this—I'm too that." God said in my soul, *Away from all of this and all of that. I brought you here! I put you here.*

It was like a tiny United Nations. We had people from all over the world on the plane. And, oh, how God had prepared one person after another! He enabled me to put links on the chain of salvation in many people's lives. Every day it was the same. I couldn't wait to get off of that pew and go get coffee. I couldn't wait to see who I would be with so that I could speak Christ into the situation with the words He would put in my mouth.

That young doctor is on his way toward Christ. Every day we sat for hours.

"I think postmodernism is dumb" I told him. We got away from talking about feeling and moved into thinking.

He would ask me, "What's the debate of the day?"

I would say, "You choose." That was very brave of me, because he might choose things that were way over my head! Sometimes it was politics. More and more as the days went on, the topic was theology.

One day he said, "I'll choose today. Why did God make Lucifer?" That became the debate for hours.

I was pushing out the sides of my soul and reaching for answers, saying, *God, I used to do this on campuses, but I've forgotten how!* I wanted Josh McDowell by my side.

What a joy to find in my total dependency and inadequacy the miracle of His words in my mouth for that young doctor; His words in my mouth for the frightened young sculpter I just loved to death who was on her way to finding Him; His words in my mouth for a family of dark-skinned people who were racially profiled even in our little group. His words in my mouth!

That is His promise. He'll give us His words along with faith enough to finish—to finish our course well and to finish strong.

PRAYER: *Thank you, Father, for giving us just what we need right when we need it.*

THOUGHT FOR THE DAY: The King of hearts in heaven promises an ongoing revelation of wisdom, because He *is* wisdom and is a giving God.

# A HAMBURGER IN THE JUNGLE

## GRACIA BURNHAM

*Praise be to the God and Father of our Lord Jesus Christ, the Father*
*of compassion and the God of all comfort, who comforts us in all our*
*troubles, so that we can comfort those in any trouble with the comfort*
*we ourselves have received from God. For just as the sufferings of Christ*
*flow over into our lives, so also through Christ our comfort overflows.*
—2 Corinthians 1:3-5

It has been a real joy for me to get to know Joyce Williams these last few years. I actually heard about her before I ever met her. When I first arrived back home in the United States from my jungle experience, the lady who did my makeup for what seemed like a countless number of television news interviews told me about her friend Joyce. Not only did I eventually meet Joyce—I'm now honored to call her my friend.

Not long ago, her church performed the world premiere of a drama about Martin's and my story entitled simply *Martin and Gracia.* We were deeply moved as the story unfolded on the stage. While we were together that weekend, Joyce told me about the idea she had for a new book about God's unfailing provision for His children even unto this day. I knew right away that the following story was the one I would tell if she asked me to contribute.

In May 2001 my husband, Martin, and I were at a resort in the Philippines enjoying a long-awaited and much-needed once-in-a-lifetime anniversary celebration. We had served in the Philippines as missionaries for sixteen years. The year 2001 had been a particularly rough year thus far, and it was so great to get away and relax.

Our exotic and romantic getaway, however, became a horrendous ordeal beyond anything we could have imagined when we were kidnapped from the resort and taken hostage by the Abu Sayyaf terrorist organization, which had ties to Osama bin Laden. Initially, we thought we would be ransomed or negotiated out in a matter of days, or in the worst case, a matter of weeks. However, our time in captivity stretched into months.

We spent our days running for our lives through the jungle as our captors avoided the Philippine military personnel trying to rescue us. We were exhausted; we starved. We slept on the ground and drank from streams and rivers. We witnessed the atrocities these men committed against civilians who lived in the villages we passed through. And time dragged on and on.

As our physical bodies weakened, so did my faith. I was shocked as I watched myself begin to question God's goodness. I started to see something in myself that I didn't want to believe existed. Where was the strong and faithful Gracia I used to know? I began to cry out to God in the midst of my faithlessness, and "the Father of compassion and the God of all comfort" (2 Corinthians 1:3) began to work in my heart.

There were days and nights when it seemed as though we could not go on. Without exception, God somehow brought just what we needed when it seemed all hope was gone and we couldn't take another step.

It was near the one-year mark of our captivity. In our worst nightmares we never thought it would last so long. Martin and I and the other hostages had lost so much weight because of our meager diet. We spent many hours talking about food; food was always on our minds. I decided to do something really wild—I asked God for a hamburger. I can't even say that I really expected Him to grant my request. I just really wanted some good ol' American food. Day after day I prayed for a hamburger.

At one point in our captivity, we were held in a small Muslim fishing village near a big city. One day a group of our captors went into the city for supplies and made a stop at Jollibee, the Philippine equivalent of McDonald's.

Late that evening the soldiers returned with hamburgers, French fries, and cokes for Martin and me. They didn't buy any for themselves, as hamburgers were forbidden. I was flabbergasted! Who ever heard of getting a special delivery of fast food in the jungle? Needless to say, it was miraculous!

We relished every tasty morsel. Isn't that just like our Lord? Even in the most horrifying situations and under the most unendurable conditions, He found a way to compensate. He gave us just what we needed—as He always does—even the most unexpected desires of our hearts as He demonstrated His love for us.

My heart, soul, and body were deeply touched with this incredible provision of our loving Heavenly Father. This miracle in the jungle reminded me of God's faithfulness and taught me to trust Him in a whole new way.

I looked back on that lesson I had learned about a month later when my dear husband, Martin, was killed in the gun battle that led to my rescue. I *knew* that the same God who had sent me a hamburger in the jungle would care for me as I went back home to rebuild my life with our children.

No situation is too difficult for God. He always finds a way to give us just the provision we need—even in the darkest times of our lives. And even when those dark times do not have the ending for which we so earnestly pray, He does provide the grace we need to keep going.

PRAYER: *Thank you, our dear Heavenly Father, for supplying just what we must have to get through the lowest points in our lives. Then you go on to give us our wants as well as our needs.*

THOUGHT FOR THE DAY: Faith makes all things possible (Dwight L. Moody).

# HIS MYSTERIOUS WAYS

## PAUL BURNHAM

*"My thoughts are not your thoughts, neither are your ways my ways,"*
*declares the LORD. "As the heavens are higher than the earth, so are my*
*ways higher than your ways and my thoughts than your thoughts."*
—Isaiah 55:8-9

My wife, Oreta, and I were excited to begin our work among the Ibaloi tribe in the rugged mountains of Luzon Island in the Philippines. We had completed our training with New Tribes Mission. Finally, God's call on our lives to take the gospel to the Ibalois was being fulfilled!

As we surveyed our needs, it was obvious that we needed an airstrip before our family could live in that village located far from the nearest road. After I found a possible site for an airstrip, I returned to our Manila headquarters to discuss our plans.

When I reached Manila, I was informed we did not have any money left in our account as our children's school bill had been paid for the whole semester. We could not get any further funds until our debt to the mission was paid, and it would be at least a month before more funds would come, as our United States headquarters sent money only at certain times.

Oreta and I were quite discouraged by this turn of events. What should we do? Nothing could be accomplished by just sitting and waiting.

I asked the mission leaders if I could borrow enough money for bus fare to return to the Ibaloi tribe to begin work on the airstrip. They agreed, so I filled my backpack with the essentials I would need for a long stay.

I walked to the bus station on a rainy, dreary day. I bought my ticket, got onto the bus, and went to find my assigned seat. It was late afternoon, and the trip would take all night. I was tired, so I was looking forward to getting some sleep as we traveled through the night.

When I sat down, I noticed that the person sitting next to me was handcuffed to the seat. My first thought was, *Oh no! Not this!* I had only a little money for food, so I knew I wouldn't be able to sleep because I didn't want to lose that while I slept. Just a few days earlier while I was on a bus, someone had slit my pocket to try to get my money. I was feeling sorry for myself. After all, I was trying to do God's work, but it seemed that everything was going wrong.

As I rode along during the night, I thought of all my options. I poured out my heart to the Lord and asked Him to show me what I should do. The bus stopped every two or three hours, and we were able to get off and stretch our legs for a few minutes. But no one ever came to unlock the prisoner who was handcuffed beside me.

Then I realized, *I may have some problems, but at least I'm free.* This prisoner had no hope. He was chained and probably going to prison. If necessary, I could write to my family, who would lend me enough money to go home. This man had no hope of escape; he needed someone with a key to unlock and release him.

The Lord was showing me that the people I was going to were in need of a Deliverer. I had the key to life—the good news of Jesus Christ. Apart from the gospel, the Ibaloi people had no hope. How could they be saved unless someone gave them the key that would free them? My self-pity turned to contentment. God was teaching me and leading us to reach those bound by Satan. The next morning I whispered a prayer for that poor prisoner who was still in chains on the bus. Then I got off and headed to our flight base.

The pilot was busy and not able to accompany me to approve the location for our airstrip. So I left my backpack at the flight base while I went to help a fellow missionary move to another station. While I was gone, another missionary saw my backpack and, thinking I had forgotten it, took it to Manila. There was no time to go to Manila as the pilot was taking his family on a two-week break. I had only one change of clothes that I had taken with me to help the other missionary. It was either wait two weeks or go on without my backpack. Maybe the Lord thought I had too much. After I prayed, I felt the Lord would have me stay and continue my mission.

The pilot and I flew over the area to look at it from the air. We found a couple of sites with possibilities. We chose one of them; then we took a bus to the place from which we could hike in to measure the site. When we determined that it would work, we got approval from the owner to use his land.

The missionary I helped to move gave me the equivalent of $30. So when I hiked with the pilot back to town, I purchased two shovels and a pick to begin work on the airstrip. The next day I hiked back to the site carrying my purchases.

I asked the village men to help me, but when they wanted to know how much I would pay, I told them I had no money, and they declined to do the work as volunteers.

The next day I began working, and for three or four days I worked alone. Several small children helped or played along with me occasionally. One day an Ibaloi man came by and saw me working and asked what I was doing. He had lived in another tribal area in a different province where New Tribes Mission was working. He began telling the people about the benefits of having an airstrip by which to take sick people to the hospital.

For the next day or two, most of the men in the village came to help. They continued working until the airstrip was finished. They brought what tools they had, and they even brought a water buffalo to drag dirt to the low places and smooth the strip.

The Lord began to perform miracle after miracle as He supplied in far better ways than I could have had I been in charge. I didn't have to worry about whether or not someone would show up to work. I ate with the people, so I didn't have to cook or do dishes. Every day someone washed my only change of clothes, so I had clean clothes to sleep in every night.

I expected it would take months to finish the airstrip, but it was miraculously completed in only a few weeks. Oreta flew in to join me, and our four children arrived shortly thereafter. We lived in a one-room house (fourteen by sixteen feet on stilts) the people provided for us. It had a five-foot ladder we pulled up every night to keep out the rats. There was only one door and one wooden window we could open during the day.

I asked the people to saw lumber for us so we could build a house. I told them I didn't have any money but that I would trust the Lord for the funds to pay them in three months. The Lord supplied all our needs. A church and two individuals whom we did not know started supporting us. A missionary from Germany paid our children's school bills.

We lived in that village for fourteen years. Oreta is a nurse, so she treated the sick—some from distant villages. They even built a house for the sick patients who needed to stay longer.

After we became fluent in the Ibaloi language, we taught the people from the Bible. We began with Genesis so they could learn who God is. Many believed on Christ as the Lamb of God, the only sacrifice God accepts for the payment of sins. Then several began to go with me to other villages to teach. They listened and watched as I taught.

Eventually nine full-time missionaries were called from that village, and they left to plant churches throughout the area.

Four of our five children have become missionaries. Although our son, Martin, died as a martyr for Christ, we do not question God's plans. Truly, our Lord's ways are higher than ours, and we know that some day we will fully understand. Until then, we will let God lead, and He continues to direct our paths through the "jungles" of our lives.

PRAYER: *Thank you, Lord, for leading us wherever we may go.*

THOUGHT FOR THE DAY: Faith makes the up-look good, the out-look bright, and the future glorious (anonymous).

# A FIRM INVESTMENT

## AS TOLD TO JOYCE WILLIAMS

*Store up for yourselves treasures in heaven, where moth and rust do not destroy, and where thieves do not break in and steal. For where your treasure is, there your heart will be also.*
—Matthew 6:20-21

I've been blessed to be dear friends with the Argabright family for most of my life. Their family is involved in missions around the world. David Argabright has many stories of the awesome experiences he and his family have encountered on more than one hundred mission trips they have led. One of my favorites is his account of the miracles God gave him on a mission trip to Argentina several years ago.

People were dying all around him. David lay helplessly in the crude intensive care ward in the basement of a small clinic in Puerto Madryn, Argentina. He had gone to Puerto Madryn with twenty other volunteers to build a church and childcare center.

Critically ill, battling a severe case of malaria, he thought, *So this is the way it ends. I'm going to die here.* He remembers praying, *God, if you don't touch me, I'll never again see the light of day.*

Visitation was very limited in the ICU, but David was thankful to God when other members of the work team were allowed to pray for him. They smuggled in bananas and Gatorade and brought his Bible to him, aiding both his physical nourishment and spiritual encouragement.

Although he was fighting delirium and hallucinations and was covered in his own blood and urine, in moments of lucidity he reflected on how the Lord called his family to be totally involved in world missions. Ironically, their commitment started with a tragic accident.

His dad, Leon, had started their family business, Argabright Contractors, in 1964. David joined the firm in June 1980. Shortly afterward, several large hospital projects began losing money. That fall one of their company vehicles was stolen. The drunk driver crashed the truck into a family car, tragically killing a girl and paralyzing her sister. Their company was sued, and the litigation lasted for sixteen months. Their lawyers told them to be prepared to lose everything.

In the fall of 1981, David's dear wife, Sharon, heard about a mission trip to the Dominican Republic. In the midst of the chaos caused by the lawsuit against their company, she said to him, "Honey, I think the Lord wants you to go." David told her she was crazy for talking like that when they were in the middle of the lawsuit, but then he thought, *If we're going to lose everything anyway, I might as well go.*

That trip changed his life forever. He loved the work in the Dominican Republic as well as the people and the services each evening. It was a great blessing to work with missionaries Dorothy and Elmer Nelson, who became like second parents to David. He was grateful that Dorothy was very perceptive, and she saw that David was a man carrying a heavy load. One night he sat despairing on the porch. Filled with guilt about the circumstances challenging their family business, he cried out to the Lord.

Dorothy came out onto the porch and hugged him. She said, "I don't know you. But I can tell you're carrying the weight of the world on your shoulders."

She shared with him that a few years earlier she and Elmer had lost their son in a motorcycle accident. Then she prayed for David and told him she and Elmer had come to love him and would begin praying for him as though he were their son. He has never forgotten her hug, those precious words, and that prayer. Since that day he has called her "Momma Nelson."

Throughout those days of hard work and nights of outdoor services the Lord continued to melt and mend David's despairing heart. Surely God had a plan for his family.

They were staying at a house near the beach. One evening David decided to walk down to the seashore. As he talked to the Lord, he knelt beside a piece of driftwood on the shore. Then, moving on and walking on that lonely beach, he began unloading everything, surrendering his guilt for the accident and what he thought was the loss of their business.

Finally he cried out, *Lord, I'm available if you want or need me. I don't have anything left to offer except myself. I love what I'm seeing here. It's so special to see lives changed forever. What I have left is all yours.*

As soon as David returned to the United States, he sat down with his dad and told him about his experience on the beach. Leon could see quite a change in David, for he had been a bit of a selfish, self-centered rascal.

David went on: "Dad, somehow I feel that God would like for Argabright Contractors to make an investment in missions." When he told his dad about the call God had given to him on the beach, without hesitation Leon replied, "If that's what you want, we'll go for it and see what the Lord will do." Just a few days later, the lawsuit was settled within the limits of their insurance policy.

They continued to work hard. Gradually, the business was revitalized as God brought new jobs their way. They kept their pledge to give to world missions—and began seeing miracles happen. Although at times they were stretched, God responded in special ways.

David's brother, Glen, joined the business a few years later, and he was in full agreement with the support of missions. Glen has participated with many of the work teams, has been heavily involved in the *JESUS* film ministry, and is a constant prayer supporter. Glen is currently the facilitator for the South Asia Partnership. These two brothers are partners in business and in ministry. Their wives, Sharon and Jeannie, have always worked right along beside them on the projects and have helped plan their mission trips.

Leon lived to see their goals fulfilled before his untimely death in the fall of 2004. They've been blessed to participate in or organize more than 100 mission trips. More than 1,000 volunteers have traveled with them, investing themselves and their resources, many of them numerous times. Some have borrowed money to fund their trips, considering it an investment with dividends that are out of this world!

These thoughts and praises ran through David's mind between hallucinations. As he remained in quarantine, with death all around him, he kept hearing a dripping sound and wondered how it could be raining in the basement. Once when he opened his eyes he could see he was covered with blood from his chest to his knees. In his hallucinations, David thought, *They've cut me in half!* Actually the blood was coming from the IV in his arm, which had popped out.

The Lord wasn't done with their family, though. Sharon came to take David home. He recovered from malaria, and he immediately began making plans for other mission trips. The Great Physician had totally restored him.

In 2004 Sharon, Jeannie, and David went back to that primitive little clinic in southern Argentina. They couldn't believe the conditions in the ICU. Only God could have brought David out of there alive.

Some of David and Sharon's greatest blessings have been working on the mission field with their children, Brad and Brittany. David and Glen's mother, Jean, is their family's prayer warrior. The blessings and eternal rewards of obedience to God's call are innumerable.

The Lord continues doing miraculous things today as Argabright Contractors continues to invest in missions and reap heavenly rewards. David and Glen are certain their dad knows all about it!

PRAYER: *Thank you, Father, for your call and your enabling resources to fulfill your plans for our lives.*

THOUGHT FOR THE DAY: To *know* God's will is humanity's greatest treasure; to *do* His will is life's greatest privilege (author unknown).

# WALTZING FROM FEAR INTO FAITH

## PATTI CAPPA

*God is my salvation; I will trust and not be afraid.*
*The LORD, the LORD, is my strength and my song.*
—Isaiah 12:2

I've often thought about the relationship between fear and faith. What's a healthy balance? It is healthy to have a good dose of fear, because that can keep us from doing some pretty dangerous things. However, if we allow our lives to be ruled by fear, we can be disabled. Fear can push faith right out of one's life. I was determined to find a way to live with both, and a crisis defined this for me.

In mid-April 2007 as I was trying to fall asleep, I had the weird thought that there was something abnormal inside my abdomen on the right side; something didn't feel quite right. A wave of anxiety and fear came over me, and I prayed, *O God, I'd better go to the doctor.*

I told my husband, Steve, the next morning that I was going to make an appointment on my next day off for a routine check-up. It would be good to have some lab work done anyway.

I continued to do normal things, including running three miles several times that week, working, sleeping, and eating. Everything seemed to be okay.

Though I felt well, I kept my doctor's appointment, and I'm so glad I did. A series of tests revealed a grapefruit-size cancerous tumor in and around my kidney called a renal cell carcinoma. The month of May was devoted to surgery and recovery. I was grateful that the cancer was contained in the kidney, and my prognosis was good. No further treatment was required, although as a cancer survivor

I'll have regular check-ups and evaluations to assure that my body remains cancer-free.

I can't explain the *why* of my experience, but I can attempt to describe it. The day before we saw the doctor, I told Steve that I thought it was cancer and that I believed the doctors would be able to cut it all out of my body.

When the doctor told me I had a tumor, my reaction was quite casual. I said, "Yeah, I figured that's what it was." Poor Steve was in shock. A few scriptures that have sustained me for several years that came to mind often during the week before surgery. I kept thinking and telling Steve, "But those who hope in the LORD will renew their strength. They will soar on wings like eagles; they will run and not grow weary, they will walk and not be faint" (Isaiah 40:31). Miraculously, I was not afraid. Honestly, I've been more afraid of public speaking than I was as I was rolled into that operating room!

I'm still amazed and blessed by this sense of peace and contentment I experienced. In pre-op I said, *Wow, Lord! I've been afraid of some pretty stupid stuff in my life, and I'm not scared now when I should be.* I can only say that even though I've faced the very real possibility of my own death—renal cell carcinoma is very lethal if it has metastasized—I'm less afraid of death than I was before my experience. I believe there will be a great big welcome for me in heaven, and that gives me comfort.

Another interesting thing happened to me during this time. Many people around the world were praying for me. I felt as if I were going into surgery flanked on all sides by prayer warriors.

I didn't ask God for much that week except comfort for my family. I recited the truths of the scripture I had in my heart, and I knew people were praying for me even when I was unable to pray for myself. It was a very humbling experience. I didn't ask God to keep the cancer contained to my kidney, though I listened to others pray that on my behalf. I simply believed that's what the surgeon would find. My job was to be as rested, calm, and well-nourished as I could be in preparation for my surgery.

One of the best things we can do with fear is let it inform us, ask why we have it, and decide if it's real or imagined and behave accordingly. I used to think my fears were pretty useless, and to be honest, most of them were.

Along the way, faith took over for me when I needed it most. The multitude of prayers on my behalf humbled me, carrying me from fear to faith.

PRAYER: *Thank you, Great Physician, for being my partner in the trials of life.*

THOUGHT FOR THE DAY: The beginning of anxiety is the end of faith, and the beginning of true faith is the end of anxiety (George Mueller).

# MATCHMAKING MIRACLE

## TINA COGGINS

*Ask and you will receive, that your joy may be full.*
—John 16:24, NKJV

If there's one thing I'm an expert at, it's daydreaming! After all, I've been doing it most of my life. As a little girl, my favorite daydream was about living in my own home with a tall, dark, handsome husband and the most beautiful baby in the world.

I pretended to be June Cleaver. I thought nothing could be grander than to be Mom to Wally and Beaver and the wife of Ward Cleaver in the sitcom "Leave It to Beaver." I could see it so clearly—pearls around my neck and not a hair out of place.

My sweetest of all havens was the persimmon tree in the pine grove in the backyard of my childhood home in South Carolina. The pine-scented woods served as a clubhouse. I was a far cry from June—a pudgy, freckle-faced, gap-toothed, stringy-haired girl—but I dreamed big. I'm sure most people agreed that I would need a huge miracle for my dreams to come true.

I accepted Jesus Christ as my Savior when I was 14. Many in my home church invested in my life, and I knew God would deliver any plan He had for my life. I just didn't know it would take so long.

There was a glimmer of hope my last year of college when I met someone who in my opinion definitely filled the bill. He was tall, dark, and handsome—and he had a desire to serve in missions in Europe. That sealed the deal for me. Surely this was it!

You can imagine how I felt when around Christmastime he said, "I've thought about getting down on one knee and asking you to marry me." I floated, the birds sang above, and I couldn't think or articulate a coherent sentence.

However, as the months went by, our conversations slowed, and the complications of a long-distance relationship began taking a toll. It slowly became obvious that he had found someone else. I was crushed, but the good that came from the experience was a seed that had been planted deep in my soul: I knew that Europe was my mission field.

Two weeks after that relationship ended, a young man visited the Christian school where I taught. Through our friendship, I was extended an invitation to live in Germany for the summer of 1985. I was privileged to live with his family and become a part of their church and travel with an evangelistic team.

I remember sitting on a train traveling through East Berlin when the Lord spoke to me about ministering in Germany. East Berlin seemed frozen in time. I saw the wall dividing the country, and I thought, *How will this huge barrier ever come down?*

I heard the Holy Spirit whisper, *Tina, this wall is nothing compared to the walls these people have built in their hearts to keep me out. Who will go in my name and help tear down these walls?*

The next Sunday a guest speaker in our church shared about mission opportunities, and I talked with him about God's call on my life. Just a few weeks later, I was at the Missionary Candidate School and was subsequently appointed as an associate missionary in Bonn, Germany. I was blessed to serve there for three years.

While in Bonn, I was reminded that nothing is impossible with God. In 1989 the Berlin Wall was torn down, and Germany was reunited. It was a tangible reminder that God brings down the walls in our lives.

Waiting is sometimes agonizing, but it also can produce an unshakable confidence in God, a strengthened relationship with Him, and the assurance that He hears and answers prayer.

While attending college in Missouri, I didn't know that my prayers for my future husband were for a man coaching just a few miles down the street. While in Germany, I didn't know that Coach

Ken Coggins was in the same country training with European and Olympic athletes. I had no idea later as I served in Teenshare, a support group for preteens and teens whose families were going through separation and divorce, that the Lord would begin equipping me to be a stepmom to Lauren.

Following the advice of my family and church staff, and at Ken's invitation, I relocated to Mississippi in December 2002. The next fall, before thousands of football fans at the Capital City Classic and the cameras of the BET network, Coach Ken Coggins asked me to be his wife. I joyfully accepted.

We returned to Raleigh, North Carolina, and on May 15, 2004, we were married. Lauren served as maid of honor, and I made my vows to both Ken and his daughter, Lauren.

With my family, I'm living my own personal miracle.

PRAYER: *Lord Jesus, thank you for giving us the desires of our hearts.*

THOUGHT FOR THE DAY: Commit thy way unto the Lord; trust also in him; and he shall bring it to pass (Psalm 37:5, KJV).

# A MIRACLE WALKING

## SANDY COMBS

*Those who hope in the Lord will renew their strength. . . .*
*They will walk and not be faint.*
—Isaiah 40:31

I've always believed in miracles. But it wasn't until I met my husband's Grandma Minnie that I began learning as a child of God that I was promised miracles in my life. Grandma Minnie believed that God could do anything.

When my husband, Bruce, became critically ill, my faith never wavered. Bruce is a farmer, and he works long hours of hard labor and is under a lot of stress. He started feeling his age when he was about 50 years old. His family has a history of cardiac disease, so he began seeing a cardiologist, hoping to discover ways he could avoid repeating the family history. He was given medical tests, but the results were negative for heart disease, so for nearly eight years he thought it was probably just stress that caused the way he was feeling.

During the winter of 2007-2008, it was all Bruce could do to make it to work and back home again. The farm suffered because of his lack of ability to lead, and we were very frustrated by the whole situation.

Then, on May 5, 2008, Bruce did his usual workout and rode his bicycle for a mile. He came in, had dinner, and sat down to watch television. Suddenly he said, "I don't feel good. I feel *really* bad. I'm sick at my stomach—I think might pass out!" Then he slid from the chair and onto his side on the floor.

I began to pray, *God, help me!* I rolled Bruce over and ran to the refrigerator for the ice pack. I placed it at the base of his head. I grabbed several pillows and propped up his feet as I dialed 911.

I looked into his eyes, which were open, but I could tell he wasn't aware of what was happening around him.

I slapped his cheek and said, "Bruce, talk to me." I could see that he was having difficulty breathing. He made a sound that's hard to describe, like wheezing but much louder. I kept slapping his cheeks and saying, "Bruce, talk to me."

As I stood over his unconscious body, I was expecting God to act, and He did.

Bruce said, "What?"

I shouted, "Thank you, God!"

Again, Bruce said, "What?"

The rescue unit arrived and checked his vitals. I could see they—like me—were greatly concerned. As I reflect back, though, I don't remember being afraid. I guess that, too, was God's hand.

Bruce spent three days in the hospital and underwent all kinds of tests. They never did determine exactly what was wrong with him, but he came home with medication for a lung infection.

After he returned home, it appeared that he was not getting better. He couldn't breathe well, he couldn't sleep, and he couldn't lie down at all. This continued for another week. When he had an adverse reaction to the antibiotic, I called the paramedics again. We had very little sleep over the next month, and Bruce's condition continued deteriorating.

Finally, on May 31 we made another trip to the emergency room. I called my sister, and she gave me the number for her doctor in Miami. After I talked with her doctor, he had Bruce transferred by ambulance to Miami so he could treat him. After arriving at the hospital in Miami, Bruce underwent another two days of tests.

One month after he collapsed, while we were sitting in his hospital room, a nurse called me into the hallway. He said, "I can't tell you anything except that we need your husband to get into bed and stay there and be very calm and remain very still."

I began smiling, and the nurse was bewildered by my reaction. I said, still smiling, "You finally found it!" It's true that God gives us calm in the midst of a storm.

Within a matter of minutes Bruce was transferred to the ICU, where he remained for three days. They administered Heparin and Coumadin, which began to dissolve three blood clots that had finally worked their way into his lungs! Many hospital staff and others stopped by to hear more about the amazing thing that was happening.

Bruce has recovered, although he still needs a lot of rest. Every now and then we tell our story to someone who hasn't heard it. Everyone who hears about it responds, "Bruce, you really shouldn't be here, you know." Bruce agrees that God must have some great things in store for us.

Thank you, Grandma Millie, for passing your faith down to us. Bruce is a miracle walking!

PRAYER: *Father, we thank you for walking with us through the dark valleys of our lives.*

THOUGHT FOR THE DAY: When we walk with Jesus, the very thing we wish for will be just what He has been waiting to do for us.

# A LITTLE GIRL'S CHRISTMAS PRAYER

## TOM CORNELIUS

*Ask and it will be given to you.*
—Matthew 7:7

It was a frosty early December morning when I walked through the door into the "His Helping Hands Ministry" area at our church from teaching a men's Bible study. As I shrugged off my coat, one of the volunteers told me a young couple had come in looking for toys for their two daughters, two and six years old. She suggested that I rummage through our "toy mountain" to see if I could find something to take out to the little family huddled in the greeting area.

Our pastor at the time, Joe Wright, had felt a burden for those who were less fortunate, so it wasn't long before our dream of beginning a compassionate ministry became a reality. Even before we had opened the doors of the ministry, the Lord miraculously gave us a flood of donated items. We received hundreds of requests every week for clothing, furniture, food, and—especially helpful in December—toys.

As I walked toward the enormous stack of toys, I thanked God for His incredible provision and the response of the warmhearted Kansans.

I rummaged through the piles of toys, but nothing seemed to be just right. There were lots of dolls, stuffed animals, and all kinds of playthings for little girls, but it was as though I could feel the hand of God leading me in a different direction.

Suddenly I remembered the big plastic toys that had been placed in a back room, because they were so cumbersome they got in the way. Moving aside a couple of plastic lawnmowers and a large, rocking worm, I came across a little pink plastic vanity with a matching chair. I just knew that was the right thing.

I hurried back to the greeting area, where the young couple were picking out some toys. I asked the mother if a large gift would be all right, and she replied, "Maybe we'd better take a look." They followed me into the back storage room. When I showed them the pink vanity set, I was amazed to see tears fill her eyes.

She said, "You must have read my mind! When our little girls saw our neighbors turn on their Christmas lights last night, they asked us if we were going to have Christmas this year. My heart ached for our daughters. Because of several really tough situations, we had to tell them that providing gifts this year would take a miracle from God. At bedtime, when our six-year-old said her prayers, she told Jesus that she knew He could do anything. In her prayer she said, 'Could you help us to share in celebrating your birthday this year?' As she was closing her prayer she added, 'Jesus, I love you, and I know you love my family. Please take care of my mommy and daddy, and let me have a pink vanity for your birthday.' I knew there was no earthly way we could get that for her.

"When I saw the pink vanity and chair, I felt I was dreaming. It was just what our daughter had described when she asked Jesus to give her something special for Christmas!"

As the young couple was loading the toys into their car, another volunteer asked them if the girls needed any clothes. They said yes but that they didn't want to take advantage because they had already been blessed so much.

The volunteer took them back to the clothing section and had them pick out some items for their little girls. Here they shared some details of their situation.

Shortly after their recent move to Kansas from California, they were in a car wreck. Because of the accident, they had lost everything they owned. The young father had cancer and was unable to work. The mother was trying to support the family with a minimum-wage job at a fast-food restaurant.

Our volunteers gathered around the couple and prayed for them and shared words of encouragement. They helped load the car with the girls' Christmas gifts as well as household items and clothing for the entire family. They even found a Christmas tree and lights.

A warm glow wrapped around us as we watched the family drive away. We had witnessed a customized miracle from the Lord! The faith of a little girl's prayer had been rewarded with God's answer to her specific request—a plastic pink vanity set!

PRAYER: *Thank you, Father, for sharing the joy of answering a little girl's Christmas prayer.*

THOUGHT FOR THE DAY: The purest faith is childlike faith.

# LIGHT IN THE DARKNESS

## JOYCE WILLIAMS

*You are my lamp, O LORD; the LORD turns my darkness into light.*
—2 Samuel 22:29

In August 2003 my husband, Gene, was the speaker for a series of meetings in upstate New York. For some reason, we experienced several brownouts and blackouts in different areas that late summer and early fall. I remember driving back to our cabin in a little golf cart in pitch-black darkness. We were very thankful for the tiny beam of light that illuminated the gravel road.

When we finally went to sleep that night, we hadn't even thought about what lights and appliances we might have had on earlier. When the power came back at 3 A.M., there were suddenly lights everywhere, and the radio was blaring. What an adventure!

The next morning at breakfast we shared experiences from our hours in the dark. As we sat around the table, the assistant to the conference leader came in and said, "You're not going to believe the story I just heard when I called back to the office in New York City." We were amazed at what he told us.

Pastor Gustavo Echeverv had traveled from Colombia, in South America, to the United States for a long-awaited visit with his mentor in New York City. Pastor Rodolfo Rivera had invited Gustavo to come to work with his people for a few weeks. So he flew into Miami and spent a few days with friends and then boarded a bus to New York City. He could hardly wait!

However, when the bus pulled into Manhattan, Pastor Echeverv soon realized something was very wrong. The streets were full of people, no traffic lights were operating, and as they rode through

Times Square, they saw that the huge neon signs were dark. The driver made an announcement, but Gustavo couldn't understand him. He kept hearing one word—*blackout*. He was dismayed to discover that the lights were out all over the city.

No working traffic lights in a city of eight million resulted in chaos. Gustavo wasn't too alarmed, however, because he knew Pastor Rivera was meeting him. He breathed a prayer of thanks.

When he climbed off the bus in front of the terminal he was dismayed, however, to find the door locked. Hundreds of people clogged the sidewalk, dragging luggage and trying to hail taxis. There was no sign of Pastor Rivera. Echeverv searched for almost two hours, but the crowd was too large. He couldn't find Pastor Rivera anywhere.

Finally he found a pay telephone and called Pastor Rivera's house. There was no answer. He was the *only* person Gustavo knew in all of New York City. He didn't know what to do. Finally, he prayed, *Lord I'm lost. I need you to guide me.*

Echeverv had one of Pastor Rivera's cards with the church's address on it, so he decided the best thing to do would be to find a cabdriver who spoke Spanish and ask him to take him to Queens. People were desperate for cabs, pleading for drivers to take them. Finally he hailed one that stopped, and he jumped into the backseat.

He asked, "¿Habla usted español?" To his enormous relief, the cabdriver responded, "Sí." Pastor Gustavo then said (in Spanish), "I'm lost. I've never been to New York before." He handed the card to the cabbie and asked, "Do you know where this church is located?" The driver took one look at the card, and to Pastor Gustavo's great joy and relief, he turned to him and said, "Of course! I know him. That's my church. Pastor Rivera is my pastor." In that city filled with millions of people, God had answered Pastor Gustavo's prayer.

As we sat at that breakfast table, each one of us shared the wonderful joy of God's answer to Pastor Gustavo's prayer. We rejoiced once again in this tangible illustration of how our Heavenly Father always provides light in the darkest moments of our lives.

PRAYER: *Thank you, Lord, for illuminating our lives just when we need it.*

THOUGHT FOR THE DAY: When God is about to do something great, he starts with a difficulty. When He's about to do something truly magnificent, He starts with an impossibility (Armin Gesswein).

# A DOORWAY OF HOPE

## CAROLE COSTA

*Because of His great love for us, God, who is rich in mercy,*
*made us alive with Christ even when we were dead in transgressions.*
—Ephesians 2:4

I never imagined that God would open the doors that have allowed me to minister to inmates at our local prison for women. It's been an unexpected mission field for me. It was a special touch of God's mercy when He crossed my path with Cheryl's, one of the inmates.

Sexual abuse began when Cheryl was nine years old, and the molestation continued throughout her teenage years. As a result, she became very angry, bitter, and filled with self-hatred. This rebellion led her down the path of early sexual activity and giving birth to a child out of wedlock when she was twenty-one.

After her daughter was born, Cheryl got married, but the marriage lasted only a few months. Life continued to spiral downward, and soon she was living with another man. She was not aware of his extensive involvement with drugs or his prior criminal record. Before long she was pregnant again and gave birth to a son.

Her baby boy was just seven weeks old when Cheryl shattered her life with a variety of wrongdoing. For the next year she found herself running from the law. Finally, she was arrested for robbery, arson, and as an accessory to a double murder. It seemed her life had come to a hopeless dead end. She wrote the about those bleak days:

> Darkness settled in all around me in that little prison cell, but the blackness in my soul was beyond description. There were no feelings that anyone loved me or cared about what was taking place. I had been sexually abused since the age of nine and was

told I was not worth anything. I felt empty, unloved, and even hated myself. How did I end up like this? Many times I wondered, *Is this all there is to life?*

Two months after being arrested at the age of 28, God brought a miracle to my life in the form of a little country preacher who came to visit me in the county jail. He told me God loved me and led me to confess my sin, seek forgiveness, and accept Christ as my Savior. I met Jesus Christ, my Miracle-worker.

Throughout that year God spoke to me as I devoured His Word, and He brought peace and healing to my life. Yes, I was still in prison physically and facing two life sentences. But my soul was free! For the first time in my life, I understood that God is a God of love, not just a God of many rules and regulations.

While serving a life sentence in prison for the past sixteen years, I've met dozens of women the world has given up on who are cast-outs. Worse yet—and this includes me—we gave up on ourselves. As I look back now, I realize that I simply existed. How can people like us ever be rescued if we don't know we're lost?

However, God very gently and patiently continued to wait for me even after I became dangerous to myself and to others. For many women, coming to a place of isolation such as prison can turn out to be a shelter from the storm and can lead to hope. I've witnessed incarcerated women recovering from various life-threatening illnesses; drug, alcohol, and sexual addictions; and others.

Nevertheless, doctors, no matter how educated and talented they are, cannot restore a soul. Only the Great Physician can heal a damaged soul such as mine. Life and all its joys are miracles every day.

It's a true delight to visit Cheryl and hear how God is using her within the confines of those prison walls. Her daily job is assisting the chaplain, helping the volunteers, and ministering to the other inmates. Many of the women seek her out to pray with them and help them study the Bible. There's no doubt that God has truly worked a number of miracles in her heart and life.

I now have the joy of being "Mamaw" to Cheryl's grandson and sharing in his life. God certainly has allowed good things to come out of a very bad, seemingly hopeless, situation.

Over time I've witnessed the miracle of a life transforming from the "cocoon stage" to developing into a beautiful "butterfly" in Christ. It's a blessing to see Cheryl share the joy of her salvation as she spreads the gospel of Jesus Christ, bringing hope to the hopeless.

Even though she's still in a physical prison, she has truly walked through the doorway of hope into life everlasting.

PRAYER: *Thank you, Father that there's no prison that can keep us from the searchlight of your love. Regardless of our past, you can make us into new creations.*

THOUGHT FOR THE DAY: It's not what we have done in our past but *who* we have in our hearts today that makes the difference.

# MEETING GOD ON THE MOUNTAIN

## WAYNE CROUCH

*Present yourself to me there on top of the mountain.*
—Exodus 34:2

*So this is how it ends. I'm going to die out here.* The pain was like nothing I had ever experienced. I clutched my chest as I lay on the dried leaves where I had fallen, deep in the Blue Ridge Mountains near Roanoke, Virginia. It was December 2004. I had hunted for years and knew it was risky to go out alone, but I had always felt somewhat invincible, not to mention that I was also very stubborn.

Conditions were great that day, and I wanted to hunt. I ended up sprawled on the cold ground—all alone. During those four or five hours as I lay there throbbing with pain, my life passed through my mind. I thought of all the bad things I had done and the people I had wronged.

I couldn't help reflecting on how foolish it had been for me to set out alone. In August 2003 I had been diagnosed with a weak heart caused by a lifetime of bad habits. My cardiologist said my heart function was so poor that I would eventually become a candidate for a transplant. To my alarm, he went on to say that replacement hearts are hard to find and most people die waiting for one. When he told me I had only about three years to live, I pretty-much resigned myself to feel horrible the rest of my days and then die.

Just a month before that day on the mountain, my next-door neighbor and I were working out in the yard. He knew about my heart problems, and he was also aware that I didn't go to church very often. During our conversation he began to talk about Jesus. For once I listened—finally! He said, "You know, if you're living for

Jesus you'll never die." Then he shared John 3:16 with me. That day he helped me learn that eternal life with Jesus could be for me. What an amazing turnaround!

First of all, I wasn't sure I believed God was real. I had grown up with my parents forcing me to go to what I called a "holy-roller" church that, frankly, scared me to death. We were "Sunday Christians." God was important on Sundays but not really talked about or thought about the rest of the week. We never prayed or lived by God's commandments. I grew up believing Christianity was like a cult—scary and hypocritical. I knew I didn't want any part of it.

With my lack of solid Christian influence, I became what might be called a hoodlum. Throughout my life I had made many bad decisions. I always felt as if life were an uphill battle. Rarely did things seem to go right for me. Frankly, there were times when I got so tired of trying and failing that I even had thoughts of suicide.

God blessed me with a godly wife, Polly Ann, who never gave up on me. Through these forty-five years, our two wonderful daughters, Missey and Cherie, along with their families and their small group at church, prayed faithfully for me. A lot of other people prayed as well. But I stubbornly persisted in doing it my way.

Polly Ann always told me that if I would believe in God and surrender my life to Him, I wouldn't be so negative. But I never felt that was an option for me. First of all, I wasn't convinced God was real. And I had done too many bad things throughout my life. There was no way God, if He existed, would forgive me.

Waves of crushing chest and back pains washed over me during those hours that seemed to go on forever. Finally I cried out, "God, if you're real, please forgive me and help me live." Right away I felt as if a weight had been lifted, and I was flooded with the knowledge that God *is* real! It wasn't long before I was able to get up and walk down off that mountain. As I walked, I thought, *God has just done a miracle in my life!*

I can't begin to tell you how much my life has changed. All the doctors have told me I should be dead. But today I'm on less medication than ever before. The guilt for the bad choices I made in the past is gone. I'm learning more about God every day. I know He has a purpose for me and that He has kept me alive for a reason.

The joy of my entire family that Sunday as I was baptized at Southside Church of the Nazarene in Richmond, Virginia, was indescribable. Tears of rejoicing flowed, and loud "amen's" were heard throughout the packed sanctuary. My ecstatic family beamed as they filled a pew. The lost one had been found!

When I wake up each morning, I thank God that He let me live to see the sun again. But I also have a deep peace that comes from knowing that if He decides to take me today, I'm ready to go. I'm amazed at the contentment that fills me.

I entered those mountains on that December day in 2004 as one person, and I came down off that mountain totally changed. I'm different now—that's what really matters.

PRAYER: *Thank you, Jesus, for mountaintop miracles.*

THOUGHT FOR THE DAY: Fear is faith in the wrong person—me! When I quit trusting myself and put the entire weight of my trust in God, He'll move the mountains in my life.

# IMPOSSIBLE!

## JUN DETALO

*What is impossible with men is possible with God.*
—Luke 17:27

It was a typical, busy afternoon in November 2006 when I saw my wife, Nancy, and my secretary entering the compound of our church and school. I wondered where they had been. I could tell Nancy was concerned about something, but I didn't have the slightest idea what it was.

She suggested that we go to our home next door to my office. When we were inside, Nancy told me that she and my secretary had just returned from an appointment with an ear, nose, and throat specialist for a checkup and that he had found a small lump in her throat. She took my hand and brought it to her throat for me to feel. I was shocked when I felt her neck. Although I couldn't see it, I could feel the growth. She said, "The doctor says I might have a goiter."

Her next appointment was set for the following afternoon. We could hardly sleep. Prayer always gives us strength and assurance that everything will be okay, but that particular night was different. We were anxious and concerned about many things, so we prayed throughout the night.

Aside from the expected financial needs we would likely experience, Nancy was very frightened about the likelihood she would need an operation. She faints at the sight of a needle, and the smell of medicine and anesthesia makes her sick. Her phobia with needles and anesthesia started when a dentist pulled one of her teeth and the numbing did not work. The dentist kept on injecting her gums while she screamed with pain. So it seemed impossible for her to face the doctor the next day.

The medical center is just a few meters away, so we walked there the next morning. The doctor, Pio Nebres, is one of the parents at our school. Nancy is his son's teacher, and I'm the school principal. He ushered us into his office and gave my wife very special care.

Dr. Nebres examined her throat and decided to excise some fluid for testing. He confirmed our suspicions that it was a goiter. Nancy was on the examination table, not realizing the doctor would use a needle to extract the fluid from the lump.

I held her hand as Dr. Nebres approached with the syringe and the needle. She was so frightened she was speechless. I looked into her frantic eyes and whispered, "It's okay—it's okay. You'll be all right." As the doctor began the procedure, Nancy passed out. He was deeply concerned and revived her a few minutes later. Finally the procedure was finished.

The laboratory report would not come for two weeks—the longest two weeks of our lives. The doctor had prepared us to be ready for surgery while the growth was still small. We spent that time praying like children, reminding God about her fear of needles and the smell of anesthesia—pleading with Him for a miracle.

Two days before the laboratory results arrived, I was amazed as my fear and anxiety suddenly went away. Peace and confidence swept over me. I knew then that a miracle had taken place. I didn't tell anyone, but I was sure our prayers had been answered.

When the day came for us to get the results, I told my secretary I already knew the results would be negative. I said, "God has answered our prayers!"

Surprised, she asked, "How do you know that?"

"God has told me so," I replied.

We went to the doctor to get the results. When he read the findings, he exclaimed, "Impossible!" He then examined Nancy's throat. The lump was no longer there. I told the doctor, "With man some things are impossible, but with God all things are possible!"

We joined hands, praising God and rejoicing. Truly we had seen the mighty hand of God at work!

PRAYER: *Dear God, help us always to believe and not to fret. May we always have unfailing faith and confidence in you.*

THOUGHT FOR THE DAY: God turns our impossibilities into His possibilities.

# THE AROMA
# OF CHRIST

## SOLOMON DINAKARAN

*We are to God the aroma of Christ among those*
*who are being saved and those who are perishing.*
—2 Corinthians 2:15

Mr. Subbaiha had a terrible skin disease all over his body. He had sores that oozed fluids that had a horrible odor. People throughout his little village near Whitefield, India, avoided him. Even his wife, children, and relatives had abandoned him. He had to stay in a separate place in his own house and was treated as though he had leprosy. He had a lonely life.

Seeking treatment and a cure, he sold several pieces of property he owned. He went to many hospitals and was evaluated by numerous doctors. Although he spent thousands of rupees, he found no cure for his dreadful disease. He was sick, sad, lonely, and without hope. As an outcast from his family and the villagers, he became very discouraged and even thought about committing suicide.

One day a *JESUS* film team came to his village. As they showed the film, Mr. Subbaiha happened to walk by and saw the crowd. He stood back but was close enough to watch the film and saw Jesus healing a blind man, raising a little girl from the dead, and liberating a young man from evil spirits. He thought, *If Jesus can heal these people, why not me?* A ray of hope came into his heart.

At the close of the film, one of the team members invited people to come forward if they wanted to know more about Jesus. He said, "You're welcome to come if you have problems, are sick, or are suffering in any way. We'll pray for you."

Mr. Subbaiah took a chance and went forward. He told the team member, "I saw Jesus healing sick people. You see, I have a dreadful, incurable disease. Do you think Jesus could possibly heal me too?"

To be honest, the team members were a little bit uneasy observing his face oozing blood and water and smelling terrible. It was a horrifying, terrible, ugly face. They did not have the faith to say to him, "Jesus will heal your disease." Yet they *wanted* to have faith enough to believe Jesus *could* heal him.

They did a wise thing. They said, "Please come with us to our pastor, Rev. D. Lazarus. He'll tell you more about Jesus and also pray for your disease."

The next morning Mr. Subbaiah went with them to Rev. Lazarus's house and met him. He said, "Yesterday I saw the *JESUS* film. I watched Jesus heal several people. Do you think He can possibly heal me as well?" Rev. Lazarus said, "Yes, I believe Jesus can heal you. So I'm going to pray for you. But before praying, let me share with you about Jesus." After he finished explaining how to become a Christian, Mr. Subbaiah knelt down and asked Jesus to forgive his sins.

Rev. Lazarus rejoiced with Mr. Subbaiah. Then he poured a little coconut oil into his hand and put his hand on Mr. Subbaiah's face. Courageously, he touched him right on the terrible sores, and he prayed fervently, asking God for a miracle. Mr. Subbaiah was so happy that Rev. Lazarus touched his face and prayed for him. It was the first time anyone had touched him in many months.

With great joy Mr. Subbaiha went home, trusting that Jesus would heal him completely.

His faith was rewarded.

Within a week the whole disease had disappeared totally from his body. The terrible secretions stopped flowing, and the odor was gone. The color of his skin changed, and slowly the scars on his body and face vanished.

All his relatives wondered about the huge miracle. When the villagers heard about his healing, they wanted to see this man who had been cured of such a horrible disease. They gathered around him and asked him many questions about how he was healed.

He shared his testimony—how he had watched the *JESUS* film. He said, "I saw Jesus healing sick people and raising the dead. And I began hoping that Jesus would heal me as well. I asked Rev. Lazarus to pray for me, and he did. He put oil on my face, and now I'm healed.

The villagers decided to call Rev. Lazarus to come to *their* village. They wanted to know more about Jesus.

Rev. Lazarus was overjoyed to have such a wonderful opportunity to share about Jesus. He presented the gospel to them, and when he gave the invitation, several people accepted Jesus Christ. The first ones to pray to accept Jesus as their personal Savior were Mr. Subbaiah's family.

Within a week, they had a worship service in their village. I was invited to go to their village to organize a congregation. I preached to a large crowd that day.

Mr. Subbaiah and his family members were rejoicing. They wanted to do something for Jesus, so they agreed to give a piece of land to build a worship center. Now Rev. Lazarus and other believers in that village are making plans to build a church there. They are currently worshiping in a public building that's actually a community hall belonging to Hindus.

It was a great day when Mr. Subbaiha and his family members, along with other believers, were baptized. They are wonderful witnesses in that village. Today that little congregation meets regularly in Mullapudi.

Mr. Subbaiha no longer exudes horrible odors that send people running from him. Instead, he shares the aroma of Christ with all who come near him.

PRAYER: *Thank you, Lord, for being our Great Physician, who heals diseases still today.*

THOUGHT FOR THE DAY: Hope is wishing for a thing to come true; faith is believing that it will come true (Norman Vincent Peale).

# HEAVENLY CONNECTION

## JOYCE WILLIAMS

*In him was life, and that life was the light of men.*
*The light shines in the darkness.*
—John 1:4-5

My husband, Gene, and I enjoyed speaking for a conference in Texas a few years ago. We were blessed as David Nixon, district superintendent for the church district at that time, shared the following story that had been told by a pastor at a denominational assembly.

Pastor Abiel Hernandez's heart pounded as the bus, loaded with over forty excited people, roared down the highway. It was exciting to anticipate that the dreams he had shared with his parents, Martin and Virginia, of starting a Spanish-speaking church in Tyler, Texas, were about to become reality.

For weeks, Abiel had driven back and forth from Dallas to Tyler looking for a place to hold services in the Hispanic community. There were lots of vacant properties, but no one was willing to make a building available to be used as a meeting place.

Now Abiel had a busload of enthusiastic people who had ridden more than eighty-five miles to help with the first service. They had been singing and laughing all the way. Abiel had not mustered the courage, though, to tell his friends there was no place to worship. To make matters worse, he had checked The Weather Channel, and the forecast called for rain. He rubbed his head as he thought about the grassy plaza right in the middle of his targeted area.

A few days earlier, when Abiel had been walking in that neighborhood, God had directed his steps to an empty church building at the end of an alley. However, it was not available. As he turned to walk away, his eyes fastened on the square out front. In that moment he could picture it crowded with people. Perhaps God had provided a meeting place without walls.

When he saw the city limits sign for Tyler that evening, somehow Abiel felt reassured that it was going to work out. He directed the driver to the square. As the bus turned down the alley, Abiel whispered another quick prayer. The driver parked the bus behind the three trees bordering the plaza.

As his friends gathered excitedly in the aisles of the bus ready to clamber down the steps, Abiel raised his voice and said, "Wait a minute! There's something I need to tell you before we get off. I was not able to locate a building, so we will be meeting this evening out here in the open. God has given us this spot for our service tonight." He quickly pushed the door open and stepped from the bus.

Without a single word of complaint or dismay, the others followed him. Immediately they began unloading the equipment and setting up the chairs. As he checked out the area, he realized that everything looked fresh and new. Tears misted Abiel's eyes as he realized that the grass on this vacant lot had just been mowed. The Lord had been preparing their sanctuary—even to trimming nature's carpeting.

As the musicians began setting up their speakers, it suddenly occurred to them that there was no place for them to connect their equipment. They began looking around, and then one of them exclaimed, "Look! You're not going to believe this! There's a silver electrical box with a two-way outlet fastened to the tree. Give me a cord. Let's see if it works."

They handed him an electrical cord, and he plugged it in. To their amazement, the lights burst into glowing brilliance in the dusky twilight. They pushed in the amplifier cord, and the speakers erupted into a cacophony of sounds. Abiel could hardly contain his joy. God was at work again—He had supplied an electrical connection!

As the singers tuned their instruments, people began gathering in that tree-rimmed tabernacle. The laughter of excited children and the barking of several stray dogs joined together in joyous harmony.

As his dark eyes glistened, Abiel and his parents watched them come, and the group from Dallas warmly welcomed everyone. He grabbed a microphone and welcomed the newcomers who had found seats. Some began clapping their hands in time with the music. What a beautiful cathedral, with the evening sky for a canopy and a carpet of fragrant, freshly mown grass!

Soon every chair was taken, and others were standing. The chords of chorus after chorus drifted down the streets and alleys, drawing people of all ages.

Abiel joyfully welcomed everyone in the name of Jesus. They listened raptly as he preached a short message and told them about God's love for them. He invited all of them to return the next week and bring their families and friends.

Just as the musicians began to sing again, a flash of lightning ripped through the sky, followed by an ominous rumble of thunder. Immediately the heavens opened, and a soaking downpour drenched everyone. Before the guitar players could get their instruments put away, they were saturated with rain. To their deep dismay, within minutes they saw that the fine woods had swollen. Surely the guitars were ruined!

As the people scattered, Abiel was deeply concerned. What could he do about his friends' guitars? They were precious and irreplaceable. Many of them had saved money for years to be able to purchase their instruments. Abiel was heartsick. They had no choice but to pack them back in their cases as best they could and load them onto the bus.

It was a subdued and soggy crowd on the bus that dark, rainy night as the glistening black ribbon of interstate unrolled before them. They were thankful for the crowd and the miraculous provision of power, but everyone was preoccupied with the tragedy of the ruined guitars. Abiel prayed constantly as his mind raced—trying to find a way to get the hundreds of dollars needed to replace them.

When they arrived back in Dallas, Abiel asked everyone to pray for an answer to the guitar disaster. Then he sent them on their way.

His heart was heavy. Throughout the night he tossed restlessly as he prayed continuously for another miracle.

Early the next morning his phone rang. It was one of his guitar-playing friends. Abiel tensed, preparing for more bad news. To his amazement, his friend said, "Abiel—you're not going to believe what has happened. When I opened my case this morning, I found that my guitar was perfectly fine. God has healed my guitar! And when I called my other amigos, they told me their guitars are fine too—just as if they'd never been soaked. Praise the Lord, brother! Your prayers have been answered!"

Abiel dropped to his knees. Chagrined that he had allowed worry to overshadow the joy of a wonderful evening, He asked the Lord to forgive him for doubting. As he knelt there, it dawned on him that the three trees bordering the square had shared a blessed secret. One of them had contained the source of power that was needed to reach the people who had gathered the night before.

Abiel was reminded of a hillside a couple of thousand years ago that had also held three trees. And the one in the middle had held the eternal connection that has illuminated the lives of all humanity through the ages—pushing away the darkness of sin's night.

When we have that heavenly connection, all things are possible. Once we plug into that source, the sky is the limit!

PRAYER: *Dear Lord, how we thank you for being the Light of the world!*

THOUGHT FOR THE DAY: Faith is dead to doubts, dumb to discouragements, and blind to impossibilities (author unknown).

# A MIRACLE BABY
## SCOTT DOOLEY

*[He] healed those who needed healing.*
—Luke 9:11

It's such a blessing to serve as a family physician and as a missionary at our denomination's hospital in Papua New Guinea, a developing country.

In October 2008 I was called to the delivery room. A mom, Cathy, had delivered her little girl at home, but the baby was not doing well, so they brought her to our hospital. I don't know how long it took them to find a car and drive to the hospital, but the baby was blue and cold and barely had a pulse when the nurses started resuscitation. When I arrived, her pulse was 60. That's very low for a newborn, whose pulse should be 120 to 160. We continued resuscitation, warming, and medicines over the next hour. I also intubated the baby.

We eventually got a better heart rate with a lot of medications, but it never got up to normal. She tried to breathe some on her own, but she had no muscle tone, and her eyes didn't react to light. I knew the baby's brain had gone too long without oxygen. Aside from breathing, there was no sign that the baby had any neurological function.

I told the parents that I had done all I could do. Then I said, "We'll pray. But we can't continue resuscitation." It appeared the baby was not going to live long unless God intervened in a dramatic way. I had been praying all along, but I felt it was time for a prayer together. I prayed with the parents for the life of their baby girl. We asked for a miracle and put her in the Lord's hands. From a medical standpoint, I knew that the baby would not live long, and if she did, she would have terrible brain damage. In my spirit, though, I felt the Lord had responded to our prayer and touched the baby.

It was a surgery day, so my wife, Gail, who is a nurse, was in the hospital since she helps during surgeries. I don't usually see her in the hospital very often, but that day she had come to find me during the resuscitation. She later said that when she walked in, she could see that it was a hopeless case and that the baby we were resuscitating was beyond our help. As she left, she, too, felt the Spirit of God checking her, reminding her that He had all power and could revive that baby. She went on her way, praying for a miracle.

When I pulled out the breathing tube, the baby continued to breathe with great difficulty, and her heart rate still wasn't quite normal. I had many other patients to see, so I left for a few minutes.

When I came back to recheck the baby, I honestly didn't know what to expect. I wondered, *Am I hearing God, or is this just my own desire to see a miracle? Will the baby be okay, or has she already died?*

I was blessed to find that not only was she still alive, but also her breathing was easier and her heart rate was normal. There was some movement in the pupils! It had been far too long for her to respond to the medicines given earlier. A little later I checked again, and the baby's pupils were normal. She was moving her arms a little and even gave a faint cry. That was a blessed sound to our ears.

My family and I continued praying for the baby throughout the night. The next day I went to check on her in the nursery. She had had a seizure during the night, and they had started her on medicines. I really felt that the Lord had answered my prayers the day before, because she improved after our prayer. Again, I laid my hands on her and prayed. When I checked her the next day, there had been no more seizures. It was a joy to hear her loud cries. She appeared to be perfectly normal.

Our family went on vacation for a long weekend. When I came back, I found that Cathy's baby girl had been moved from the nursery to the ward to be with her mother. She was breastfeeding well; she had no more seizures or any other problems and was off all medicines.

Later I saw a Christian lady we know in the hospital. She had also just delivered her baby. She wanted to know more about the "miracle baby." She said Cathy was still telling everyone about the way God had healed her baby girl. I was deeply touched when they told me they had named her Sylvia Scott after me.

That little baby girl is truly a miracle from the Lord. Today she's very active and appears to be perfectly healthy. Sometimes a cry is a miracle.

PRAYER: *Thank you, Lord, for your healing touch.*

THOUGHT FOR THE DAY: More things are wrought by prayer than this world dreams of (Alfred Lord Tennyson).

# MY CHAINS FELL OFF

## BETH ELLENBERG

*My tongue will tell of your righteous acts all day long.*
—Psalm 71:24

On March 21, 2004, I was singing in the church choir when I began experiencing what I thought was a migraine headache. I had been having migraines for about fourteen years. This time, however, it was different. A blood clot on the right side of my brain had broken communication with the left side of my body, causing a stroke that left me paralyzed.

Although the outlook was grim, God gave a promise to me not to worry about anything—that I would be totally healed.

I began having home health care for physical and occupational therapy three times a week. After three months, I regained some movement and strength in my arm. However, my leg had no movement and very little feeling from the thigh down. Without the help of braces on my leg, I was confined to a wheelchair. I had been told by my neurologist that I would never walk without the aid of a straight brace to stiffen my knee, because I had no use of the muscles that caused my knee to bend.

After three more months of outpatient therapy, I was told there was great concern because there was no nerve or muscle movement. I continued to go on the faith that God had promised He would heal me so I would get back to 100 percent. The therapists continued to work hard with me, even beginning water therapy, which caused tremendous pain and spasms. I continued the electric shock therapy three times a day as well.

Finally, on Wednesday, September 15, the therapist tried to re-move the braces from my leg and ankle to see if I could bear any weight on my left leg. As three of them stood holding me, I stood and shifted my weight to the left side. When I did, my foot rolled to the side. Even with the therapist trying to hold it in place, it could not support me. She replaced the ankle brace, and with her assistant and another therapist on both sides of me holding my knee straight, I was able to bear weight on my leg for short periods of time. I believe God orchestrated this plan for that particular day, because it would further prove what He was about to do. No one would be able to say it was therapy that healed me.

We were in revival at our church, and I was scheduled to sing the next day. As I got up to sing, wearing braces on my leg and ankle and holding to a walker, my pastor said, "I wouldn't be surprised if God healed Beth in this revival." When he spoke those words, my heart leaped. But as I sang, my face began to droop and draw, making it hard to get the words out. The pain in my body intensified. The words of the song pierced my heart, and I had a yearning to "be more like Jesus" as the song said. Throughout the remainder of the service, I just wanted to get alone with God and pray. I went home with a stirring in my soul that I could not explain. I decided to spend the next day in prayer.

As I started praying, I began by just thanking God for the deep desire for prayer, because throughout the past six months it had been a struggle to pray. Although I had felt God near and sensed His love and provision in an awesome way, I had not spent much time in prayer. It was as though God was carrying me through those difficult times. I knew He had been asking me to step out in ministry, but I was so afraid to do that—I couldn't even walk! So I just kept putting it on the back burner and thinking I would deal with it later.

Finally, I knew I had to settle it. I had come to realize that God had *allowed* the stroke for my *good* in order to demonstrate His power. As I continued to pray, I began asking God what He wanted from me. He began showing me things He wanted to change in my life, making it clear that what really matters is living for Him and leading others to Him. I agreed to everything He showed me and continued in a spirit of prayer.

When I had first started praying, I was impressed to take off my braces, but I didn't want to take the time. Again I heard "Take off the braces." I tried to ignore it. Then as I said to God, "What do you want of me?" I heard again "Take off the braces." Finally I said, "Yes, Lord," and immediately threw them off. I felt a release.

To my absolute amazement and inexpressible joy, I stood and walked across the room! It was as if the stroke had never happened. My foot and leg were strong, and I could move them in any direction. I had been reading from the Psalms. I looked down at my Bible, and my eyes fell on Psalm 71:24: "My tongue will tell of your righteous acts all day long." That was what I was going to do! I couldn't wait to tell someone what had happened.

I went to see my husband and my daughter. Then I visited the place where I had been having outpatient therapy. What an awesome day of witnessing and rejoicing! Even the therapists admitted it was a miracle. They told me that even if the muscles and nerves had simply been awakened, they would have been very weak.

After a full day of running around witnessing about my miracle, I returned home and dressed in my new four-inch heels I had bought especially for my 100-percent recovery. That night we returned to church for another revival service. When I walked into the sanctuary, as Pastor Dave said later, "Holy pandemonium broke out!" People began shouting and praising the Lord. They just couldn't believe it. The night before, I had stood before them wearing braces on my leg and foot and holding myself up with a walker as I sang. Now I was running around in high heels, kicking up my feet and marching around the church.

Many people came to pray at the altar seeking God before the message began. Pastor Dave said he believed that was the reason for my healing. Many others came to know Christ through my healing, including my therapist and my father. But I knew God wasn't finished. He had brought me to a place of complete, radical surrender. I was finally ready and willing to be used by God in whatever way He desired.

In the eight months following God's touch, I shared my testimony at many churches in eleven states. I've since answered a call to ministry. Everywhere I speak, I see people touched by the fact that God still performs miracles. I've seen souls saved and people return to the Lord after years of falling away. I've seen sick people healed because their faith was increased when they saw and heard what God has done for me. It is a wonderful thing! I'll never understand why He would do such a great thing for me, but I'm so thankful to be used in such a way.

Doors began opening for me to speak for revivals, women's retreats, marriage retreats, and prayer seminars. God has now placed me in a pastorate where He continues to use me to reach others for His sake. Many times when someone needs counseling, my story is the basis for assuring them of God's power to do whatever is needed in his or her life.

I would not want to have another stroke and put that tremendous burden on my family again, but it was worth the suffering to see God move in such a mighty way. Most of all, I thank Him for keeping me through it all.

I can sing with that old hymn "And Can It Be?" written by Charles Wesley in 1738, *My chains fell off; my heart was free / I rose, went forth, and followed Thee.*

PRAYER: *Thank you, Jesus, for your healing touch.*

THOUGHT FOR THE DAY: Our main business is not to see what lies dimly at a distance, but to do what lies clearly at hand (Thomas Carlyle).

# A SON OF GOD

## WORKU GEREMEW

*To all who received him, to those who believed in his name,*
*he gave the right to become children of God.*
—John 1:12

"You are no longer my son!" Those harsh, angry words from my father devastated me. He was angry and embarrassed, because the principal of my school in Addis Ababa, Ethiopia, had told him, "I have been in this school for eleven years, and I have not seen a troublemaker like Worku." My father's outraged response chilled my heart.

My younger brother and I had a very difficult childhood. Our mother died shortly after my brother was born, poisoned by her own brothers and sisters because they wanted a piece of land she owned. Our father was stern and never showed much tenderness toward us. After he made the harsh declaration renouncing me as his son, I felt like an orphan.

He had raised us in the Ethiopian Orthodox Church, which was filled with superstition and guilt, so I didn't perceive God as a loving father full of grace and mercy. All I felt was fear and hopelessness. It was almost unbearable to continue living at home.

Not long after my father rejected me, I attended a service at an Evangelical church. I listened intently as the pastor read John 1:12—"To all who received him, to those who believed in his name, he gave the right to become children of God." I was riveted by those words. Instantly, I knew that I had found my Heavenly Father to replace the earthly father I had lost.

Without hesitation I went forward and surrendered my life to Christ. My heart was warmed as I was covered by His forgiveness and love. I knew my Heavenly Father would never reject or forsake me.

From that moment on, I was on fire for Jesus. Nothing could squelch my passion. I enrolled in a Bible college in Addis Ababa. It wasn't long before I realized God was calling me to spread the gospel.

Once again my father was very angry and did not approve of my breaking away from the Orthodox Church. He threw me out of the house. That didn't slow me down—I stayed with friends, but many times I was uncertain about where my next meal would come from.

After graduating from college, I enrolled in a seminary in South Korea, where I completed my master of divinity degree. Then I returned to Ethiopia, where I helped plant many churches. I preached all around the area and taught at the college from which I had graduated.

The Holy Spirit began speaking to me about my anger toward my family for killing my mother. I knew I had to forgive them. God miraculously gave me the grace to go to my uncle and tell him that I forgave him and the family for what they had done. By relinquishing my anger toward them, an even deeper peace settled over me.

In 1999 I had to leave Ethiopia because of the unrest there. I lived in Washington, D.C., for a year and then went to Covenant Theological Seminary in St. Louis. The Lord directed me to New City Fellowship Church, where, as I listened to the pastor's messages, I learned even more about God's grace. I became involved in the church's immigrant and refugee ministries.

That was when the Lord defined His call on my life to be a bridge between the "new Americans" and established citizens. I spent all my extra time with families who had relocated to the United States from around the world. As a fellow immigrant, I understood their struggles.

It was during this time that I met Rebecca, and she became a special friend. She shared my passion for racial reconciliation and meeting people's basic needs. It wasn't long before we fell in love and married.

The Lord led us to begin Rise Together Ministries to bridge barriers between races as well as to share the gospel. We also partnered The Well Community Church, a new church plant that pursued the goal of introducing people to Christ by meeting their basic needs. We've established a furniture ministry, tutoring and mentoring program, GED training, and job development. One of our newest visions is to establish a charter school that focuses on immigrants and refugees for whom English is a second language. Our goal has been to open the school by 2010.

Recently I returned to Ethiopia for the first time in nine years. It was a joy to share the country of my birth with Rebecca. Our dream and prayer is to start an orphanage there.

The joy of the Lord permeates every aspect of my life as I trust Him to help us accomplish all He calls us to do. God always comes through, even when we seem to have no funds or help. That's why my faith in my loving Heavenly Father never wavers. He never lets us down.

PRAYER: *Thank you, Father, for your unfailing love.*

THOUGHT FOR THE DAY: Love so amazing, so divine, demands my soul, my life, my all (Isaac Watts).

# THE MIRACLE
# OF A FLOWER

## KENDRA GRAHAM

*See the lilies of the field, how they grow.*
—Matthew 6:28 (KJV)

On June 27, 1996, I stood on the big iron railroad tracks just outside Salzburg, Austria, admiring the beauty of God's creation. On that radiant summer day, the majestic, soaring mountains overlooking the vast rolling valley were filled with trees and wildflowers bursting forth in vibrant colors. It was breathtakingly beautiful.

As I glanced down at my feet, trying to keep my balance on the iron track, my heart began to ache as my thoughts wandered to the past. In front of me was an exclamation mark to God's awesome creation. But behind me stood the stark reminder of one of the most horrifying acts ever committed by humanity—the Nazi concentration camp Mauthausen.

Those iron tracks had brought trains filled with God's chosen people as well as enemies of the Nazi regime to unspeakable torture and death. I imagined the creaking of the wooden railcars and Hitler's officers yelling as they herded people off the trains.

As I passed through the gates, my spirit was deeply troubled. To my left was a building with a solid wooden door. Inside were the well-appointed barracks of Nazi soldiers. There was even a small pool where the officers could swim. Conveniently located next to them were the buildings that had housed the female captives. Our guide said, "Those officers raped and abused those prisoners at random." My stomach twisted.

The next building was where the German officers herded the prisoners like cattle and then forced them to strip. Their valuables were placed in a heap for the officers to rummage through and choose what they wanted for themselves. From there we were led to the showers where prisoners of all ages bathed together. If the prison was overcrowded, some were gassed upon arrival. Others were even burned alive. In the basement I saw the ovens where the bodies of the dead were cremated. It seemed as though I could still detect the stench of burned flesh.

Overwhelmed with grief, I almost fell to my knees, not believing people were capable of such evil. I continued on through the barracks, reading that hundreds slept together in tiny, vermin-infested quarters—adults, children, and infants crammed together.

Outside, I breathed deeply as I felt anger welling up within me against such ruthless tyranny. There's no explanation for such evil except that sin has been present ever since the fall. My heart raced with anger.

As I began praying, God calmed my heart. He reminded me that He's still in control. I cried out within my soul, *I know you're all-powerful, but where were you? I don't see you, Lord, not here, not in this place of death and despair.*

I felt God leading me to leave my group and walk to the huge stone wall surrounding the camp. It was at least seven feet high and had three feet of barbed wire along the top. I knew that prisoners had been lined up there and shot execution-style. Through the barbed wire I could see freedom. How dreadful it must have been to see freedom so close yet unattainable! I could almost feel the hopelessness of the people who once inhabited this prison.

As I knelt there, looking down through my tears, splashes of color caught my eye. The most delicate, intricate, beautiful flowers—yellow, purple, and white—were blooming inside those walls of horror! Those gorgeous flowers were proudly blooming with strength and beauty in a place engulfed with indescribable evil.

I wondered, *Why? Why, Lord, would you allow something so beautiful to exist amidst this horror? This place, Mauthausen, does not deserve such beauty! Lord, why didn't you curse this land by not allowing anything to grow here, not a flower, not a weed, not a blade of grass?*

In that still, small voice, He whispered deep within my soul, *Dear child, when will you learn? Not even the most horrid and cruel of all evils can stop me! My light will always pierce the darkness. I'm always near!* Suddenly I felt His love and compassion manifested through that garden by that fence.

Those beautiful, fragrant flowers were emblems of hope through the barbed wire and pain. I pray that those long-ago prisoners had seen such blooms and were somehow reminded that God's beauty will not be destroyed.

The faint whistle of a train brought me back to reality. It's true—we will never understand such atrocities and blatant evil. But may I always remember the miracle of these flowers blooming where despair had once reigned.

PRAYER: *Thank you, Father, for your beauty that blooms in the midst of sorrow.*

THOUGHT FOR THE DAY: There's not enough darkness in the world to extinguish the light of one small candle.

# A SPARROW'S REST

## JOYCE WILLIAMS

*A lowly little sparrow*
  *Soaring high up in the air*
*Never worries, doubts, or frets,*
  *For he trusts our Father's care.*

*Though buffeted by storms*
  *He rests safely in his nest,*
*Not worried or filled with fear—*
  *For his Creator knows what's best.*

*Peace fills that tiny bird,*
  *A miracle in all life's storms!*
*For he's sure our Father's love*
  *Will keep him safe and warm.*

*Lord, may I, like that sparrow,*
  *Hold tight through every test.*
*Then when storms blow through my life,*
  *I'll find peace and your sweet rest.*

PRAYER: *Thank you, Heavenly Father, for providing a safe haven in the storms of our lives.*

THOUGHT FOR THE DAY: Look at the birds of the air; they do not sow or reap or store away in barns, and yet your heavenly Father feeds them (Matthew 6:26).

# TAKING JESUS AT HIS WORD

## NINA GUNTER

*Jesus replied, "You may go. Your son will live." The man took Jesus at his word and departed. While he was still on his way, his servants met him with the news that his boy was living. When he inquired as to the time when his son got better, they said to him, "The fever left him yesterday at the seventh hour." Then the father realized that this was the exact time at which Jesus had said to him, "Your son will live." So he and all his household believed.*
—John 4:50-53

Every child is a miracle from God. My husband, Moody, and I taught our two sons, Dwight and Dwayne, to believe in the awesomeness of God, the Creator and Sustainer of life. We intentionally talked about and modeled before them a strong faith in the grace and wisdom of God's will. Our goal as a family has been to walk consistently in love and obedience to God.

We prayed with our boys daily and made a conscious effort to remain alert for opportunities in everyday, ordinary happenings to initiate meaningful conversations that would testify to God's work in our lives moment to moment.

In 1983 our younger son, Dwayne, then 17, contracted an unknown illness following a hunting trip. Our first suspicion was flu or a short-lived virus. However, his condition worsened as he began experiencing high fever, chills, muscle aches, and breathing difficulties.

Soon it became evident that I must take him to the emergency room of a hospital in Columbia, South Carolina, where we lived. After examination, he was admitted to the hospital. The doctors were not certain what Dwayne's illness was but diagnosed it as pneumonia. Despite their treatment, he continued getting worse.

One night he aroused from a drug-induced sleep and recognized me standing by his bed in the darkness, praying fervently for God to guide the doctors to a successful diagnosis and treatment. Conscious of my prayers, his faith increased. He later told us that he knew God would work a miracle of healing for him.

After several anxious days, Moody and I moved Dwayne to a hospital in Charleston, South Carolina, where a Christian doctor and friend joined us in prayer. He was divinely guided to a diagnosis related to Dwayne's hunting trip. He told us Dwayne was suffering from tularemia, also known as rabbit fever. With this accurate diagnosis came an effective treatment. God was at work!

We learned anew that miracles grow out of difficulties. Every daunting situation is waiting to become a possible miracle.

Later we discovered that at the most critical time of Dwayne's suffering, a group of ministers and their spouses had conducted an all-night prayer meeting, interceding to God for healing. The doorway for the release of God's power was opened.

The Bible gives us guidance on how to pray for healing:

Is any one of you sick? He should call the elders of the church to pray over him and anoint him with oil in the name of the Lord. And the prayer offered in faith will make the sick person well; the Lord will raise him up. If he has sinned, he will be forgiven (*James 5:14-15*).

Today Dwayne and his beautiful family love and serve God with strong faith.

We find peace in every crisis throughout our lives when we expect God's intervention. We can rest in His answer—whatever that might be. This is "the peace of God, which transcends all understanding" {Philippians 4:7).

PRAYER: *Dear Heavenly Father, please give us the faith we need to expect your answers to our prayers. Then help us to remember to acknowledge them and thank you when they come.*

THOUGHT FOR THE DAY: There is only one thing that will save us in the hour of desperation, and that is prayer (Stephen Olford).

# FREE AT LAST!

## BRIAN HELSTROM

*I, the LORD, have called you in righteousness; I will take hold of your hand. I will keep you and will make you to be a covenant for the people and a light for the Gentiles, to open eyes that are blind, to free captives from prison and to release from the dungeon those who sit in darkness.*
—Isaiah 42:6-7

"I know it's difficult for you to believe, but I have to tell you that the pastor of this church has served time in prison," said the *JESUS* film team member. He went on to say, "His story is a great testimony of God's grace and divine providence." He then told us the story.

The Caribbean area is scattered with numerous islands—some of which provide better living conditions than others. It had been a blessing for the team to show the movie in several locations, especially the day they went out to a town on one of the islands to show the *JESUS* film.

It was a particularly difficult city to enter because of political unrest. They were looking for a location to show the film, and finally found a kind woman with a small house that had a big patio. After explaining to her about the *JESUS* film and telling her they wanted to show the movie to the people in her area, she very graciously gave permission to use her patio. Then she began telling her friends and neighbors about the showing. There was a buzz of excitement throughout the area.

The evening the film was shown was a truly blessed time. It seemed as though the Lord had especially poured out gorgeous weather. Filled with anticipation, excitement, and curiosity, people from all across the area gathered on that big patio. They chatted excitedly as the film began to roll. Then they were quiet, totally absorbed in watching the flickering images on the screen.

At the close of the showing, there was rejoicing when several of the viewers came forward to pray to accept Jesus as Lord. One of the new believers was the hostess, and the team was especially blessed to pray with her for her salvation.

During the prayer time, she asked them to pray for her husband who was in prison. As a new believer, it was her desire that he would also find, as she had, forgiveness, peace, joy, and a personal relationship with Jesus.

After several days of ministry in that area, the team left. But they continued praying for those new believers. They had a long list of special prayer requests—including the husband who was serving time in prison.

Some months later the *JESUS* film team returned to the island and visited that city. To their joy and amazement, they found the patio that had once served as a viewing site for the *JESUS* film had been enclosed, and the new addition was a church!

The team was overjoyed. When they knocked on the door, their kind hostess came to greet them. When they inquired about the church and other changes, she joyously exclaimed, "Oh Yes! God has been *so* good to us. We have many new believers."

Then she said, "I want you to meet my husband—the one for whom all of us had been praying." He came up behind her, and she said, "I have the blessing of presenting my husband to you. He is now the pastor of our church!" They knew they were experiencing a miracle from the hand of God!

The team was to meet with many of the people who had come to know Jesus the night of the film showing on the patio who are now members of the rapidly growing church. There were many new believers there who had come to know Christ as a result of the ministry of the *JESUS* film and there were many stories of intervention by the Lord.

That evening, as the team met with the new believers for their service, they were overjoyed to hear the message delivered by the former prisoner whose heart is now captivated by the kingdom of the Lord. He's spreading the good news to all who will listen.

They believe completely that this pastor and his congregation have been freed by our Savior, Jesus Christ, to serve in the army of the Lord!

PRAYER: *Thank you, Lord, for coming to set captives free.*

THOUGHT FOR THE DAY: Prayer begins where human capability ends (Norman Vincent Peale).

# A PERFECT MATCH

## PHYLLIS PENNINGTON HILL

*We ought to lay down our lives for our brothers.*
—1 John 3:14

As I watched my grandson, Alan Pennington, walk across his high school platform to receive his diploma, I was filled with joy. I reflected back to those frightening days that began when he was just seventeen months old.

Because he had chronic ear infections, Alan had surgery to put tubes into his ears. The anesthesia from what should have been a routine procedure seemed to precipitate alarming responses. Alan quit walking, talking, and rolling over. He just lay listlessly in his bed, crying constantly. Within days he had lost eight pounds. He just wasn't himself anymore. His parents were at their wit's end.

Alan's dad was in the army, so his parents took him to Womack Army Community Hospital for a battery of tests. He was given antibiotics for the ear infection, and he seemed to get a little better. But suddenly he got much worse and was rushed to the emergency room. After a battery of tests, the initial diagnosis was meningitis. Another round of antibiotics soon had him back to his playful, happy self.

Then Alan's parents began to notice that he was unsteady, fell often, and was becoming less responsive. He had a seizure and was rushed to the hospital again.

The doctors were at a loss. As his temperature rose, he became more and more lethargic. More tests were run, and one of the scans revealed a shadowed area in his brain. Alan was immediately taken by ambulance to North Carolina Memorial Hospital in Chapel Hill. He was in a coma by the time they arrived.

The doctor who examined him there said, "I can almost bet this little guy has leukemia." That diagnosis was confirmed, and our hearts were gripped with fear. Specialists who were called in explained to us that the leukemia had weakened Alan's immune system, causing the infections and fevers.

After treatment with the six strongest drugs available, Alan finally went into remission. He steadily improved for several weeks, then relapsed. After several days of treatment, he went back into remission. His hair began falling out. I flew to be with Alan and his family, because in addition to coping with Alan's illness, they were expecting another child. It also really helped me to be able to hold, rock, and read to our very sick little boy.

The doctor told Alan's parents that his best chance for survival was a bone marrow transplant and added, "The best donor would be a sibling; that would give him a one-in-twelve chance of success." We felt that God could be answering prayers through the new baby girl who was on the way. When Amanda was born, tests showed she was a perfect match! The greatest challenge was to keep Alan alive until she was big enough to donate the bone marrow.

Unfortunately, Alan went into his second relapse right after Amanda's birth. Although the doctors gave him the strongest drug available, it didn't work. They hammered him with other drugs and more radiation until he finally went into remission once again. However, the doctors warned that Alan could have stunted growth, mental impairment, and other handicaps. It was a frightening time for all of us.

Finally Amanda was four months old, and Alan was well enough for the transplant procedure. Soon after arriving at the University of Minnesota Hospital, treatment was started to get Alan ready. The risky procedure began as the doctors harvested one cup plus one teaspoon of marrow from tiny Amanda.

We gathered around Alan and prayed as he was given the bone marrow. When Amanda woke up, she had a happy smile on her little face, as though she knew she had done something great. She went home that afternoon.

Alan remained in a sterile environment for several weeks. Finally he returned home to North Carolina on Labor Day weekend. What a happy day!

Watching Alan get well was the witnessing of a miracle unfolding before our eyes. He seemed to regain strength almost hourly.

It has been a great joy to celebrate many milestones with Alan over the years. One of the highlights was his wrestling on the school team—pinning three guys in one tournament. Alan might be small, but he's mighty!

When Alan's name was called and he walked across the platform to receive his diploma, it was not a routine high school graduation. We clapped long and hard, beaming with pride as we watched. Another wonderful milestone in his young life was reached when he left for college in the fall of 2006. The gift from a tiny baby sister has reaped countless rewards. And they've only just begun!

PRAYER: *Thank you, Lord, for your faithfulness in walking with us through the trials of life.*

THOUGHT FOR THE DAY: The gift of life is a gift that keeps on giving.

# FROM WHOM ALL BLESSINGS FLOW

## JOYCE WILLIAMS

*Blessings crown the head of the righteous.*
—Proverbs 10:6

It's always amazing when the Lord intersects our lives in ways we don't anticipate. A few years ago I was having lunch with a group of ladies at Trevecca Nazarene University in Nashville, where my husband, Gene, was serving as pastor in residence. To my surprise, after a few minutes of conversation I discovered that one of the ladies at our table was a distant cousin of mine.

Another time, I was scheduled to speak to a group of ladies at a luncheon in St. Joseph, Missouri. While eating lunch with several of the ladies, I discovered that the lady sitting across from me, Judy Richmond, had lived in my hometown of Roanoke, Virginia, for several years.

She and I talked about Roanoke—where I had lived and where she had lived. Then I asked, "What church did you attend?" When she said, "Parkway Wesleyan," I got really excited and said, "That's Uncle Lewis and Aunt Hallie Hunley's church!" I told her about singing in that church with my sister when we were kids. It was amazing to continue sharing overlapping memories.

Judy said, "You know, I remember hearing a story about your Uncle Lewis."

I just love hearing stories, so I said eagerly, "Please tell me!"

Although Uncle Lewis had gone to heaven a number of years before Judy and Tom moved to Roanoke, she said they still heard stories about him and dear Aunt Hallie. She said, "Pastor John Ott frequently talks about a critical meeting one night that resulted in a real turning point for the church."

She continued: "The church—it was then called Fallon Park Wesleyan Church—was in serious financial crisis. The pastor called a meeting and shared the critical concerns. The situation looked hopeless, and they wondered how they could go on. Bills were due, but there was no money to pay them. They prayed, but no answer came.

"Then all of a sudden a deep, resonating voice began to sing spontaneously,

*Praise God, from whom all blessings flow.*
*Praise Him, all creatures here below.*
*Praise Him above, ye heavenly host.*
*Praise Father, Son, and Holy Ghost. Amen.*

"That was your Uncle Lewis! As the amen resonated, the atmosphere in the room began to change. Expressions of gloom and doom were replaced with hope and expectation as faith kicked back in. The simple but incredible message of that old hymn and the confidence of that faithful patriarch permeated the chambers of their hearts. Their hopelessness turned to anticipation. It wasn't up to them! All blessings *do* come from our Heavenly Father. So why not praise Him in advance? And that's just what they did. They stayed there and prayed together, joyously celebrating what the Lord was going to do."

Judy and I praised God together. Our Heavenly Father had once again used an aging saint and an ancient anthem—written in 1709 by Thomas Ken—to restore faith and hope. She went on to tell me, "They say it was almost as if tangible showers of blessing were raining down from heaven on them. They prayed and rejoiced together, basking in those precious heavenly moments. No one wanted to leave.

"From what they tell us, that evening was a miraculous turning point. The church leaders determined that by God's enabling leadership and provision they could do whatever was necessary to keep the ministry going. It was God's church. He would bring the resources. And He did!

"With the foundations of their faith firmly attached, they proceeded with relocation plans. They stepped out on faith and purchased eighty-six acres of prime property in a strategic location near the Blue Ridge Parkway. They began to build, and they changed the church's name to Parkway Wesleyan. Their tiny landlocked church building was sold. As God had promised, resources came in to meet every need.

"In 1987 Parkway Wesleyan moved to their new location. Today approximately 1,100 people worship there each Sunday. Multiple ministries are available to people of all ages. It is surely a lighthouse in that community! And they're still praising the God, from whom all blessings flow."

PRAYER: *Father, may we have the faith to see beyond the impossibilities of the moment and look ahead to your provision for tomorrow.*

THOUGHT FOR THE DAY: Prayer is a powerful thing, for God has bound and tied himself thereto. None can believe how powerful prayer is and what it is able to effect but those who have learned it by experience (Martin Luther).

# COME-TO-THE-FIRE MIRACLE

## ALETHA HINTHORN

*The people were amazed when they saw the mute speaking,*
*the crippled made well, the lame walking and the blind seeing.*
—Matthew 15:31

When Dottie Bartlett's daughter invited her to attend the 2008 Come to the Fire conference in Olathe, Kansas, Dottie's first thought was *How many pills will it take to get through all three days?*

Dottie had been in an accident at work in 1997 that had injured the rotator cuff in her right shoulder as well as a disc in her neck. She was in constant pain. Physical therapy, muscle relaxers, medications, and even surgery did nothing to relieve it. It hurt to stand, to sit, and to lie down. When she did manage to sleep, she dreamed of pain.

As a result, Dottie became depressed. All the things she loved to do—hold her grandchildren, sew, knit, needlework, give and get hugs—hurt too much to do. Joy and happiness were being wrung from her life.

She had always known that God could heal. She had seen her Grandpa Chappell healed after having all his bones broken when he was crushed into a sand road under a massive earthmover. She had seen her Uncle Melvin survive life-threatening injuries and fevers after being hit by a speeding car. She had seen her Grandma Boosinger survive being struck by lightning that melted the hairpins in her hair and the nails in her shoes. Each time, doctors said, "It's a miracle. God is the only answer."

Yet Dottie had been afraid to ask God for her own healing. She thought, *What if I'm not worthy and He doesn't heal me?* She had put a protective shell around that fear and her heart.

In each of the Come to the Fire conferences, we have a healing service for women who need healing either emotionally, physically, or spiritually. During that Friday afternoon healing service, Dottie felt the protective shell fall away. For the first time, she was ready to ask for healing from a God she knew loved her unconditionally and could and would heal *her*.

Dottie later said, "I wasn't healed right then, but I felt in my heart that I would be healed before Come to the Fire was over."

On Friday night Joy Griffin shared her story of healing from excruciating pain that had lasted for months. Dottie knew she must speak to Joy and ask her to pray for her healing.

At the close of the conference, Dottie went to her, and Joy prayed. Dottie believed that God had used Joy as a conduit and that they had prayed in one accord. There were no immediate signs, but in her heart she knew she was healed.

Dottie said, "The next morning I got out of bed and was halfway up the hall before I realized that I had actually *gotten out of bed!* It had taken me twenty or thirty minutes to get out of bed for the past eleven years! I raised my right arm above my head! I could hug my husband again without pain. The constant, unbearable pain was gone! You can't imagine the joy that welled up in my heart! I couldn't wait to tell every one about the miracle God had done for me."

If anyone asked her how she felt, Dottie said, "I feel great, because God healed me!" Her husband, her daughter, and her church family rejoiced with her. They could see the joy in her eyes and in her smile. They saw her raise her arms in praise to God.

The running joke became "Dottie, can you still raise your arm?" They knew she couldn't before, and now they shared her joy.

"The pain is gone. The anxiety is gone. The depression is gone," Dottie reports. "I can carry my youngest grandchild without worrying that I might drop him. I can knit again. I knitted two shawls in one week when it had taken me a month to make one before! I can do my housework again. Even that is a joy!

"I look forward to each new day to see what God has in store for me next. I praise Him with my voice, my heart, and my soul.

His miracles are for today, and I'm honored to be living proof of His mercy and goodness.

"Every day I'm reminded by little things I can do—holding a sewing needle, picking up a penny on the counter, brushing my hair. Every day is filled with beauty again. I can ride to church as well as make the seventy-five-mile trip to see my family for our monthly dinners with joy, not pain.

"This is truly a miracle, and I have pledged to devote the rest of my life to serving Him!"

PRAYER: *Thank you, dear Jesus, that by your stripes we are healed.*

THOUGHT FOR THE DAY: We must begin to believe that God, in the mystery of prayer, has entrusted us with a force that can move the heavenly world and can bring its power down to earth (Andrew Murray).

# HIS GLORY REVEALED

## GEORGE H. HUNLEY II

*I consider that our present sufferings are not worth comparing
with the glory that will be revealed in us.*
—Romans 8:18

Bad news seemed to have become the defining factor in my life. I became so accustomed to hearing it that I found myself walking about with a sense of impending doom, worrying about my next catastrophe. I never, however, allowed myself the luxury of questioning God's will for my life. I knew that since He is God *of* my life, He would continue to be God *over* all my circumstances. Therefore, I rested on His promises.

Then, at the age of 35, I suffered a stroke. I began a regimen of 32 pills per day for anxiety and depression, high blood pressure, diabetes, heart disease, and emphysema. Some of the illnesses were due to heredity, but most were caused by my lifestyle before I met Christ. In 1981 He delivered me from years of drug addiction and gloriously saved my soul. Then He called me into the ministry.

I reasoned that God was not in it—these illnesses were my fault. My health demanded that I leave the ministry and move back into my childhood home in Louisa, Virginia, with my three sons.

I had no means of financial support, and I was imprisoned by all those pills, seven inhalers, a nebulizer, and oxygen twenty-four hours a day. I knew I was slowly dying. My only hope was that God in His infinite mercy would intervene and permit me to see my sons grow up. But that was six years away. At the rate I was declining, I knew I wouldn't survive that long.

I wholeheartedly believed Philippians 1:21—"To live is Christ and to die is gain," but the parent in me desired to be with my sons long enough to see them through their childhood, grounded in life, and living with faith.

After subjecting me to every possible test and treatment, my cardiologist sat me down in his office. Holding the multitude of test results in his hands, he spoke these words to me: "George, you're going to have to get used to the idea that you'll be dealing with this for the rest of your life." In light of the new blockage in my heart, the scar tissue, and the congestion, my death was quickly approaching.

I scheduled angioplasty/bypass surgery, rewrote my will, and determined to spend all my remaining time with my sons. We had been staying at my parents' home for the two weeks prior to my surgery, because my condition had deteriorated to the point that I was completely bedridden.

On the day before my surgery, I asked my parents to take us to our home church in Louisa. I wanted to be with my church family one last time. With everyone gathered around me, my pastor, Dan White, anointed me and prayed for God's healing. I was absolutely convinced that God *could* perform this miracle, but I wondered why He would. After all, I had done this to myself! So I was very nervous going into the hospital Monday morning.

When they rolled me through the doors of the operating room, I felt a sense of impending doom and panic. In my fear, I believed I would not come out of there alive. The assurance that He was still Lord over all and was still on the throne was all that consoled me.

I lay on the cold, steel operating table that morning and whispered a simple prayer of submission to His will over my life or death, whichever was His perfect plan. When the cardiologist inserted the catheter into my artery to review the blockage, the monitor screen showed that the scar tissue, the blockage and the congestion around my heart were *no longer there!* I was not only alive, but God had healed me!

My heart was new. The oxygen tank, along with all of the medicines, went straight into the trashcan, where they belonged. The Great Physician had taken away my old, worn-out body and made it like new. My illnesses were instantly wiped away. I went home that evening and held my three boys as we thanked God for His divine healing, mercy, and grace.

It has been more than seven years since that glorious day. My sons are grown and living on their own. I'm married to Christie, a wonderful Christian woman, and am blessed with three fantastic stepchildren. I'm back in the ministry, and God is still Lord of my life.

As I settle in at the end of a busy day, I recall the promise that God whispered to me when I was on that operating table: *I love you, George, and I'll always be with you. Not only will you live, but you'll live to see your grandchildren grown.*

I did not deserve this great gift from God, but He loved me so much that He sent His only Son to Calvary to suffer so that I may be healed—in every way. My life's theme is "I'd rather have Jesus than anything this world affords today."

I have this message for my former cardiologist: "You're not going to be able to count on me for your retirement income. The Great Physician has taken over my case!"

PRAYER: *Father, thank you for your blessings, for the love of those you've given me, and for the privilege of each day you allow me to serve you.*

THOUGHT FOR THE DAY: A day filled with God's love and grace is better than a lifetime of the treasures and comforts of the world.

# AT EVERY GAME

## KAREN KINGSBURY

*No eye has seen, no ear has heard, no mind has conceived*
*what God has prepared for those who love Him.*
—1 Corinthians 2:9

In the town of Bakersfield, California, was a seven-year-old boy named Luke who played baseball on his town's little league team. Luke was not very talented athletically, and he spent much of his time on the bench. Still, Luke's mother, a woman of deep faith, attended every game and cheered for her son whether he struck out or not.

Life had not been easy for Luke's mother. Sherri Collins was in college when she and her longtime sweetheart married. They lived what seemed like a storybook life until the winter when Luke was three years old.

On an icy highway, coming home from a second job he worked at night, Sherri's lifetime love was killed in a head-on collision.

"I'll never marry anyone else," Sherri told her mother. "No one could ever love me the way he did."

"You don't have to convince me," her mother responded. The older woman was also a widow, and she gave Sherri a sad, understanding smile as she said, "Sometimes there's just one special person for a whole lifetime. Once that person's gone, it's better to be alone than try to replace him."

Thankfully, Sherri was not alone. Her mother moved in with her after the funeral, and together they cared for Luke. No matter what trial fell upon the young boy, Sherri had an optimistic way of looking at it.

"That's okay, son," she would say when Luke came home sad about a situation with a friend. "One day he'll realize how much fun you really are, and then he'll be knocking at the door every afternoon."

Or she would encourage him when he struggled with learning to read. "You can practice reading to me every night, Luke," Sherri told him. "Won't that be a nice way to spend time together?"

Sherri had something deep within her that many mothers understand—an ability to recognize the speed at which time passed. Knowing it was flying by didn't make it any easier to stop, of course. But for Sherri, it meant making the most of every moment. More than anyone else, she knew how quickly things could change.

When Luke turned seven and joined the town's little league team, Sherri sensed from the beginning his struggle.

In an effort to make things right for him, she researched stories about major leaguers who struggled with the game when they were kids.

"Did you know that the most famous infielder of all time didn't play a lick of ball until he was twelve?" she told him. And together they would laugh over the possibilities. "One day I'll be cheering from the stands, and there you'll be—suiting up for the big leagues."

Game after game, week after week, his mother came and cheered him on—even if he played only a few minutes at a time.

Then one week Luke came to the game alone.

"Coach," he said, "can I start today? It's really important. Please?"

The coach pondered the child before him and thought of Luke's lack of coordination. He would probably strike out and swing at every ball that came his way. But then the man thought of Luke's patience and sportsmanship during the weeks he had played but an inning or two.

"Sure," he said and shrugged, tugging on Luke's red cap. "You can start today. Now go get warmed up."

Luke was thrilled, and that afternoon he played the game of his life. He hit a home run and two singles, and in the field he caught the fly ball that won the game.

The coach, of course, was stunned. He had never seen Luke play so well, and after the game he pulled him aside.

"That was a tremendous performance," he told the child. "But you've never played like that before. What was the difference today?"

Luke smiled then and the coach could see his childlike brown eyes welling up with tears.

"Well, Coach, a long time ago my dad died in a car wreck. My mother was very sick. She was blind, and she couldn't walk very well. Last week she died." Luke swallowed back the tears and then continued. "Today—today was the first time both my parents got to see me play."

PRAYER: *Thank you, our Great Physician, for your ultimate healing.*

THOUGHT FOR THE DAY: How far away is heaven? It's not so far as some imagine. Those who are full of the Spirit can look right into heaven (Dwight L. Moody).

# FAITH IN ACTION
## RANDY LEDSOME

*Why all the commotion and wailing? The child is not dead but asleep.*
—Mark 5:39

On July 3, 2008, I received an urgent call from a member of our congregation. "Pastor, my nephew's wife went in for a routine weekly checkup. As you know, their baby is due in a couple of weeks. During the examination the doctor found that the baby is in distress. So they rushed her to the hospital for an emergency C-section. When the baby was born, he wasn't breathing and didn't breathe for fifteen minutes until they were able to resuscitate him. Pastor, they really need someone. Can you come?"

She informed me that they were taking the baby to Women's & Children's Hospital in Charleston, West Virginia, but his mother would have to remain at Thomas Memorial Hospital in South Charleston. I rushed to the neonatal ICU. Since there was no family member to authorize me to go in to see the child, I waited outside for one to arrive.

Suddenly a nurse came rushing down the hallway asking, "Is there a minister here from Elkview?" Although my church is in Charleston, we live in Elkview. When no one else moved, I acknowledged her call. She led me back to the infant, explaining the baby's hopeless situation.

She said, "We, the nursing staff, want you to pray for this baby." I told her I would be glad to. Several of the nurses gathered. We laid hands on the tiny baby, and I prayed. Then I went back to stay in the waiting area until the father arrived.

When he and his mother got there, we were allowed into the cubicle to watch as they attempted to save that precious tiny baby.

Finally I returned to the waiting room to meet with other family members as they arrived.

As they gathered, I explained that the baby was in critical condition and on a ventilator. He had been given medication to force his little heart to beat. If they were able to stabilize him, he would most likely end up at the hospital in Pittsburgh.

While I was sitting there, a nurse from our church who had just come on duty came running down the hallway and mouthed to me, "He's coded again!" I followed her back to the neonatal ICU. I found the doctor shouting out instructions and doing compressions on the baby's tiny chest. After at least fifteen minutes, he turned to the father and said, "We can't do any more. It's for the best that we let him go. Otherwise there will be much too much brain damage."

I confess that my faith was shaken. But "faith in action" took over. When the tiny infant's father heard those words, he became as limp and frail as the baby. I held him in my arms and prayed as he wept for the loss of his baby boy.

The nurses proceeded to disconnect all the lifelines that had sustained the baby for those few short hours. The doctor placed the call to the mother to tell her what no parent ever wants to hear and letting her know that they had done all they could do.

The nurses got a handmade crocheted blanket and cap, made with love and prayers for times like these, wrapped the baby in them, and handed him to his dad and grandmother to hold him for his last remaining moments. His blood sugar count was 4, and his heart rate was 18. It surely would not be long. The color began leaving his face. As I watched them hold the baby, I prayed, and I thought, *What if it were my child?* I could feel their grief.

Another ten minutes ticked by. Once again, the doctor checked the baby's pulse and breathing. He explained to the family this was probably for the best since the baby had been deprived of oxygen at birth and then a second time. He explained the medication would cause his heart to beat a few more minutes but that it would finally stop, and he would be gone.

Another fifteen minutes passed, and the doctor checked the infant again. He looked puzzled. Then he left the room to instruct the nurse to place the baby back on the monitor. We followed them back to the tiny bed and watched as the nurse reattached the monitor and then placed him in an oxygen tent. To our great joy, within minutes his heart rate was 140, and he was breathing completely on his own!

The respiratory nurse came to witness what was happening. Word was quickly spreading throughout the hospital that a miracle had taken place. Hospital personnel were all well aware of the fact that you can't just remove the ventilator. It must be done gradually. By human standards it's impossible—but our God specializes in the impossible.

As the baby's vital signs continued to stabilize, the doctor said, "I can't explain what's happened—it shouldn't be." Then he called the baby's mother at Thomas Memorial Hospital to tell her, "Your baby boy is alive!"

A few days later, Baby Cameron left the hospital with his mom, dad, and big brother. There was not a dry eye that morning as they walked through the doors tenderly holding a tiny miracle.

PRAYER: *Father, may we dare to believe you to do the impossible in and through our lives.*

THOUGHT FOR THE DAY: We find firm footing when we step out on God's promises.

# THE GIFT OF LIFE— RETURNED

## LORRIE LINDGREN

*He stilled the storm to a whisper.*
—Psalm 107:29

It was the week before Christmas 2006, and we were caught up in the usual hustle and bustle of the holy season. The highlight of this time each year for us is the chance to be with extended family from out of state.

Even though our home in Denver is the center of family activities during holidays, I needed to make a quick trip to Bakersfield, California, to introduce Women of the Harvest at a Christmas brunch. The temperature was in the sixties on Tuesday when I left for California, so I didn't take a jacket. I had no way of knowing Denver was about to experience three blizzards in less than three weeks.

After visiting with the guests following the brunch, I was escorted back to the Bakersfield airport. When I checked in for my flight, they told me it had been cancelled due to a blizzard in Denver. I had been so distracted with the holiday activities that I was not even aware that a storm had been predicted. The agent told me I could not reschedule a flight home until Christmas morning—five days later!

I began checking into other options. To my amazement, God miraculously got me on a fifty-passenger plane to Colorado Springs that same night—although I was number twenty-two on the standby list. I felt so unworthy that I should get on a flight when thousands of passengers were stranded in Los Angeles. *Why me, Lord?*

It was still a treacherous flight. Colorado Springs was experiencing the same blizzard as Denver, and it was a difficult landing. There were only two brave cab drivers to transport passengers to nearby hotels. Visibility was very limited. I felt relieved to reach the warmth and safety of a hotel.

The blizzard continued to howl until noon the next day. I extended my hotel stay through Friday, expecting the interstate to Denver to reopen the following day. But it actually opened around 5 P.M. when one narrow lane was cleared. Jim, my husband, made the icy drive to Colorado Springs to rescue me. We finally got home late Thursday night.

As I jumped back into the Christmas activities, I continued to thank the Lord for the gift of being home with my family, knowing that thousands of people were still stranded. On Saturday morning, December 23, I made a quick grocery store run to get last-minute ingredients for the holiday meals.

When I returned, Jim told me he had been having pressure in his chest for about half an hour. I suggested he call 911 even though he was sure it was just indigestion. He preferred to call the doctor's office and not bother the paramedics. He told me that one of the employees of the doctor's office had said to come to their office to be checked. Later we learned they told him to call 911, but apparently his brain wasn't getting enough oxygen, and he had heard what he wanted to hear—instructions to go to the doctor's office.

When we pulled into the parking lot at the doctor's office, Jim began vomiting, and it finally clicked. Chest pain and nausea are a bad combination. I ran inside for help. They did an EKG and immediately called for an ambulance; he had been having a heart attack for about sixty minutes by that time.

Jim was given nitroglycerin and put on oxygen. But his heart stopped before the paramedics got there. The doctor began chest compressions with no success. When the ambulance arrived, the paramedics intubated him. They worked for forty-five minutes to resuscitate him and find a pulse, using the paddles three times. I found out later that they seldom try for more than twenty minutes on an adult.

Finally, after Jim had been clinically dead for forty-five minutes, his heart began beating irregularly. They transferred him to a gurney, but his heart stopped again during the ride to the hospital. It was Saturday, and the heart catheterization lab team was on call. By the time they arrived, Jim was too unstable to move up to the lab.

We waited another fifteen or twenty minutes as they worked to raise his blood pressure so he could be moved upstairs. We were invited to come to his bedside to say our good-byes. His heart stopped again during the procedure, but a stent was successfully inserted.

In the cardiac care unit one of the doctors gave orders to cool Jim's body temperature to ninety-one degrees during the first twenty-four hours following surgery to help his neurological system recover. This procedure had been used for a couple of years to help brain injury patients and had recently been tested on patients who experienced cardiac arrest.

Twenty-four hours later, they began to warm Jim's body back to a normal temperature. They checked him to determine whether he would be able to tolerate having the ventilator removed, then asked me to step out of the room while they removed the breathing tube.

When I was allowed back in, Jim's eyes were open, and he asked, "What am I doing here?" The doctor standing by Jim's bed wept as he told me we were receiving a miraculous Christmas gift. He said, "This never happens. People just don't survive what your husband went through." The doctor had expected Jim not to live through the first twenty-four hours and anticipated that if he did live he would be severely brained damage or paralyzed. Jim was neither.

I am in awe of God's precious gifts to us that Christmas. I love to share the story of the many miracles we witnessed within a few days. God knew that I needed to be in Denver and prepared the way for me to be by Jim's side to receive the second two gifts.

More than two years later, Jim is doing great. He has modified his diet, and he exercises six days a week. His last checkup showed that he's doing well. He was released from his doctor's care a year after his heart attack. He has a slight memory loss that is hardly noticeable.

We praise God for the precious gift of life.

PRAYER: *Father, thank you for the many gifts we receive from your loving and gracious hand.*

THOUGHT FOR THE DAY: Afflictions are but the shadow of God's wings (George MacDonald).

# MIRACLES IN THE WAREHOUSE

## JANICE LONG

*You will be my witnesses.*
—Acts 1:8

My new job working in a warehouse was quite different from what I had thought I would be doing. My husband, Miles, and I had sensed God was releasing me from continuing my ministry to children and their families through my home-based daycare center. I had different ideas about my new venture.

However, we felt very clearly that this warehouse job met all of the criteria we had laid out; it was part-time, flexible, and with no nights or weekends. It offered just the income we needed. God had whispered in our hearts, *This is it!* We believed it was where He wanted me to be.

When I walked in on my first day, I realized immediately that I had been sent to quite a mission field! The profanity was awful, and my coworkers seemed to have sad lives. It broke my heart to see such hopelessness all around me. I started praying each morning that God would somehow make me a shining light in that warehouse. I asked Him to give me opportunities to share my faith and testimony.

At that time my job involved putting price tickets on merchandise. So my coworkers and I had all day to talk and build friendships. As time went by, I noticed that people were trying not to curse around me. Some even began apologizing for outbursts even though they had not been directed toward me.

I remember one incident in my first year when two men got into a profanity-laced argument. I ignored them and went on with my work. Later one of them came to me and apologized, saying, "A good

Christian woman like you wouldn't want to hear that." I was surprised and honored that he respected me and Christianity enough to apologize. We had spoken only casually, and I had never shared my faith with him. But he knew.

People came and went at work, and I continued to have opportunities to talk about some of the things God was doing in my life. As we worked together, our conversations turned more and more to the Lord. One day a new friend told me she had never worked in a place where God was mentioned so often. She thought it was a very positive thing.

Some of us moved on to different jobs as time went by, but I noticed that things had changed. For the most part, coworkers stopped swearing when I was with them. A feeling of family had begun to replace the pervasive hopelessness.

Laure, one of my new friends, went to her homeland in Brazil to visit for three months. Her marriage had been falling apart, and she wanted to be with her family. When she returned to work, her face was radiant as she hurried toward me. She said, "Now I know what you were talking about! I accepted Christ as my Savior while I was in Brazil."

Her new-found peace and joy radiated from her like a wildfire as she bubbled over with the love of the Lord. Her young daughters were saved soon afterward. She committed to putting her marriage back together, and a couple of years later her husband was saved. They're hoping to return to Brazil and begin a ministry there.

After Laure's conversion, it seemed that the Lord really began working in that warehouse. Others were saved and began growing in the Lord. Vanessa, one of the young Christians, suggested we start a Bible study during an extended lunch hour one day a week. We rejoiced when upper management gave us permission, and we soon began to average from four to twelve in our group.

When we heard that a Billy Graham crusade was coming to our area, we decided that our Bible study group would all go to the Friday night service. It was really fun to ride together on my church's bus.

I was especially glad that Mary joined us. Although she had attended some of our Bible studies, she usually, as she said, played the part of devil's advocate. It was obvious that she was hungry and searching. She listened intently to the message, and when the invitation was given, she went forward and accepted Jesus as her Savior. The bus ride back to the church was filled with praises as we rejoiced in Mary's new birth.

Julie, my supervisor, had been with the company for ten years when I first started working there. She had a foul mouth and was hard to get close to. As things started changing at the warehouse, I noticed a difference in her. Then I found out that she had become a Christian as well. The walls started coming down as the Lord became the focus of her life. It has been like watching a butterfly come out of a cocoon. She later went on a mission trip to Kenya.

Because of some new rules, we had to move our Bible study offsite, but God is still working in many lives. Anthony was a young man who visited our Bible study a couple of times but had been reluctant to give up his lifestyle. We heard that he recently gave his heart to the Lord and was baptized.

When Julie and I talked not long ago, she told me that what they had needed in that warehouse was a mentor—someone who would show them how to live a godly life—and that she believed God had sent me to them. I was humbled and praised God for His perfect plan.

When I look back over these years, I can't put into words what God has done around me as He has poured out His love and mercy in that workplace. Lives have been changed and are still changing. I get a daily dose of encouragement and blessing as we share what God is doing in our lives. What started as a tiny flame has become a huge bonfire of miracles shining with the love of Jesus throughout that big old warehouse.

Thank God for putting me in an unlikely mission field—right where He could use me.

PRAYER: *Father, may I always be a beacon of your love shining in the dark world around me.*

THOUGHT FOR THE DAY: Do all the good you can, by all the means you can, in all the ways you can, in all the places you can, at all the times you can, to all the people you can, as long as ever you can (John Wesley).

# A DIVINE APPOINTMENT

## PAULA MARTIN

*Even though I walk through the valley of the shadow of death,*
*I will fear no evil, for you are with me.*
—Psalm 23:4

My husband, Jerry, was driving as we barreled across Interstate 40 in late December 2008. We were headed for a short New Year's Eve ski vacation in the mountains with our son, Bill, and his family one thousand miles away. We had enjoyed a wonderful Christmas with family and friends, complete with lots of calorie-laden and sugary goodies.

Jerry's cell phone rang as we were approaching Albuquerque. It was a nurse from the doctor's office back home. Jerry had not been feeling very well, so we had gotten him in to see a new doctor for some lab work when his regular physician was not available.

The nurse told Jerry that everything looked pretty normal except that his cholesterol was high and he needed to start taking medication to lower it. We told her we were traveling and would be home the following Monday.

Because his dad had been diabetic, Jerry asked about his blood sugar level. She looked through the report and gave us the reading. When we asked if that wasn't really high, she said she would check with the doctor and call us back. Fifteen minutes later she called and said the doctor wanted us to stop at a pharmacy in Phoenix and contact him so he could call in a prescription for a medication to lower his blood sugar level. We later discovered there had been a computer error that had missed the high reading.

It was a relief to find a pharmacy near the interstate. We decided to purchase a meter to see if the high reading might have been an error. As we talked with the pharmacist, a man who had just completed his purchase overheard our conversation. He said, "I don't want to interfere, but that reading is much too high. You need to check your levels right now, because you could go into a coma or worse."

He showed us how to use the meter and get an accurate reading. Then our new friend said, "My name is William Summers. I'm a physician. You should go to the emergency room at the nearest hospital, which is just two miles away. But you might have to wait quite a while since it's a holiday. Why don't you call your doctor again?"

We reached the same nurse, and Dr. Summers talked to her and pulled out his pad and starting writing prescriptions for Jerry's high blood sugar and cholesterol as requested by the nurse. We asked him if he would talk to our daughter, Julie, who is registered nurse. They talked on the phone and agreed that Jerry should start taking insulin immediately.

We were amazed when Dr. Summers took Jerry into the men's room and showed him how to use the syringe to inject the insulin. He spent at least forty-five minutes with us, asking Jerry questions and giving us information about diabetes. We discovered that Jerry had experienced some key symptoms—weight loss, thirst, and frequent bathroom stops. He had also had recent changes in his vision and had just gotten a stronger eyeglass prescription.

As he left, Dr. Summers gave us his business card with both his cell phone number and home phone number on it. He encouraged us to stay in the area near the hospital and call him in an hour with Jerry's readings. We thanked him profusely and told him our meeting at the pharmacy counter had been orchestrated by God. He said, "God has a funny way of bringing people together."

After he left, the pharmacist said, "Dr. Summers is brilliant— one of the top physicians in our area. He actually discovered a drug that's used to treat Alzheimer patients!" We were in good hands.

An hour later we called Dr. Summers with Jerry's reading. He told us it was still much too high and recommended that we stay there near the hospital. Then he told Jerry how much insulin and medication to take on a sliding scale. He said, "Eat a good supper, and call me in the morning before you leave town."

We stayed in a nearby motel, and after a restless night we called Dr. Summers the next morning. He talked with us for about forty-five minutes—on New Year's Day! Jerry's reading was considerably lower, and Dr. Summers said it was probably safe for us to travel.

We drove on to meet our son and his family at the remote ski resort in Arizona. Following doctor's orders, Jerry didn't ski, but he enjoyed watching the grandkids and telling them about our miraculous encounter. Then, exhausted but feeling blessed, we drove to Phoenix that night. His sugar levels stayed lower.

Dr. Summers called again the next day to check on Jerry. We insisted he send a bill for his services, but he said all he wanted was a call telling us Jerry's blood sugar levels were under control.

With many prayers, we got back on the interstate to head home a couple of days later. It began to snow and sleet as we approached Flagstaff, Arizona. There were many wrecks all around us, but once again the Lord watched over us.

With the stress and driving hazards, Jerry's sugar levels began climbing, so we spent the night in Amarillo, Texas. We were so thankful when we reached our home in Wichita, Kansas. Our Good Shepherd and Great Physician had guided our steps—leading us to a divine appointment at that pharmacy counter.

PRAYER: *Thank you, Father, for guiding us—even when we don't know we're in trouble.*

THOUGHT FOR THE DAY: The steps of faith fall on the seeming void and find the rock beneath (Walt Whitman).

# DYING GRACE
## JOYCE WILLIAMS

*Precious in the sight of the LORD is the death of his saints.*
—Psalm 116:15, KJV

I went to be a comforter—I came away comforted.

Forrest Newlin, a dear friend and member of the church my husband pastored, had been sent home from the hospital. He was dying. It was a very sad time for our church, because Forrest was much loved by everyone who knew him.

The Lord impressed upon me to take lunch to the family. His sister-in-law Maxine opened the door. I handed her the bags of cheeseburgers and fries I had brought for the family. While they ate, I joined Shirley, Forrest's daughter-in-law who is a nurse, as she tenderly cared for him. In the midst of her grief for their imminent loss, a sweet serenity bathed her face.

When Shirley told Forrest I was there, he blinked his eyes in acknowledgment. Deeply moved, I tenderly held his hand.

I recalled many acts of kindness this gracious, gentle man had performed over the years. I had personally witnessed many of them; some I had heard from others. His genuine love and concern for everyone were innate parts of who he was. God and everyone else knew they could count on Forrest.

Pulling myself together as best I could, I took out my New Testament and began to read familiar passages of comfort. In his fading capacity, Forrest responded by slowly, almost imperceptibly, nodding his head. The Shepherd I was reading about was walking with Forrest and his family through the valley of the shadow of death.

Doris Betts stopped by for a few minutes on her lunch hour. She sang "What a Friend We Have in Jesus," Forrest's favorite song.

It seemed we could almost hear the faint echo of angel voices as she sang those precious words. We saw the shadow of Forrest's familiar smile lift the corners of his mouth as he listened.

The Holy Spirit was there—waiting to escort this faithful one across the finish line.

Several times it seemed as if Forrest was gone. There was no discernable movement of his chest. The only way I could be sure he was alive was by watching the faint throb of the pulse in his neck. I wondered what he was seeing as he laid there poised for that final heavenly flight. Perhaps he was touching two worlds and had already glimpsed some heavenly wonders.

I had some questions for him; there were messages I wished I could give him to take to my own loved ones who are in heaven. Then I remembered: they already know—no longer in part—the whole story! For them the darkened glass has been illuminated, and they are seeing "face to face" (1 Corinthians 13).

As I gently rubbed lotion into those frail hands and onto his face, I again sensed a response. His hand grasped mine tightly as he slipped into a peaceful slumber.

In those tranquil moments the Holy Spirit began to minister to me. Troubles, pressure, and crisis upon crisis had taken their toll. But in that quiet place I found a calm oasis for my stressed-out soul. Again I echoed the familiar passage in Psalm 23:3—"He restores my soul." Even in the dark valley of near-death, our Father had paused to touch my soul as well. Knowing Forrest as I did, I wouldn't have been surprised to hear him say he had been lying there praying for all of us.

When his dear wife and son returned from making arrangements at the funeral home, I shared 2 Corinthians 1:3-4 with them: "Praise be to the God and Father of our Lord Jesus Christ, the Father of compassion and the God of all comfort, who comforts us in all our troubles, so that we can comfort those in any trouble with the comfort we ourselves have received from God."

God had used this precious man on the brink of heaven to bring solace to all of us in our time of sorrow and grief. I felt my heart lift as I said good-bye. I had witnessed a miracle of dying grace.

I had gone to be a comforter, but I left with repairs made to some holes in my soul.

PRAYER: *Father, may I be your witness in my final hours.*

THOUGHT FOR THE DAY: A saint is one who makes it easy to believe in Jesus (Ruth Bell Graham).

# MIRACLES IN THE ROUGH

## KIM MCLEAN

*Many of the Samaritans from that town believed in him
because of the woman's testimony.*
—John 4:39

I thought life was over for me—at least life as God intended it to be. Through unrealistic expectations and poor choices, my life had become a burden rather than a gift.

I grew up in North Carolina in the Bible Belt. To me, being a minister was simply a given. For as long as I could remember, I had loved Jesus. I had read my Bible faithfully from the time I was ten years old. I had musical gifts, so I had learned piano, guitar, and composing.

The overwhelming message I garnered from my family and community was that a girl's priority should be physical beauty so that she could find a good husband to please. It was a flawed lesson in economics at best, and a travesty as it played out in my life.

At age sixteen I was a sophomore in high school, a straight-A student with big musical dreams, a call to the ministry, and an engagement ring on my finger. I was married shortly after graduation, the same year my parents divorced.

It was not unusual in our family to marry so young, especially for the women. So I was set—first order of business covered. There was no need for college, because I had a husband. One dream had come true, and I began praying for the rest. *Lord, I'd like to have two little giggly girls, and I'd like to be a professional songwriter.* I imagined God jotting down my order and running back to heaven's workshop to get on with fulfilling my plans.

I've always been a bit of an idealist, a hopeless romantic. Nonetheless, family issues from my childhood began surfacing. Addiction began taking over my life as I struggled with an eating disorder—anorexia.

My husband had his own family-of-origin issues to deal with, but we allowed the good times to outweigh the bad for a while. We had been married four years with still no little girl when I learned that my low weight was causing infertility. I began praying for a miracle, and a year later our first daughter was born.

I did a great deal of self-directed study, mostly music and theology, and I began hungering for a college education. I auditioned at the University of North Carolina Greensboro and was accepted as a piano/composition major, but I was too sick with anorexia and had to withdraw halfway through the first semester. Another miracle happened the following year, though, when our second daughter was born.

I had become a prolific songwriter. My husband took me to Nashville, where we learned that my songs were competitive in the market and that there could be plenty of money involved.

We moved our family to Nashville, and I signed a publishing deal a month later. "God is speeding my plans right along," I reasoned. Then my husband quit his job to find his own dream, but it would be some time before I was making enough money to support a family by myself.

As my husband and I grew apart, I became sicker, and he became resentful. I ended up in the hospital with anorexia and bulimia and nearly died. We had no health insurance, so it was a blessing when the treatment center gave me a full scholarship.

Recovery was long and grueling, but the treatment saved my life. Unfortunately, my soul went numb. I had been drifting from God, and I began falling into lonely traps, trusting the wrong people, and making my colleagues my family.

My husband and I separated and then divorced. I had never experienced being single, and I went wild. I was miserable, terrified, and covered with shame. I lived a dual life, trying to be a good mom to my girls but attempting to stay numb with alcohol and relationships.

Then one day I remarried. It was just that quick. Too ashamed to turn to God, I turned to the only other strength I knew—a husband. I was unfaithful and ruined, and that resulted in another divorce after we had been married for just one year.

The following year I met my third husband in the music industry. Another new identity. I was his fourth wife. We had a son—a gift from God. Our marriage, however, could not withstand our pasts or the tension of two teenage daughters who felt let down and confused. After seven years that marriage, too, ended in divorce.

I had great career successes, winning awards and nominations as a songwriter, recording albums of my own, and producing records. But my family was broken.

Finally I turned back to God full-throttle. I took back my maiden name with a vow to follow God's plan instead of my own. I went back to school. Four years later I received a bachelor's degree. One and a half years later I completed my master of arts degree in biblical theology.

Since placing all my expectations and hopes in the Lord, my life has become a gift rather than a burden. Psalm 62:5 has become a life verse for me: "Find rest, O my soul, in God alone; my hope comes from Him."

I'm like the woman Jesus met by the well. He told me all I've ever done, and He set me free. I'm not ruined—I'm His minister. And that's a miracle!

PRAYER: *Thank you, Father, that you still set captives free.*

THOUGHT FOR THE DAY: Above all the grace and the gifts that Christ gives to his believers is that of overcoming self (Francis of Assisi).

# WHAT HAPPENED TO MY MIRACLE?

## HOLLY MILLER

*My thoughts are not your thoughts, neither are your ways my ways.*
—Isaiah 55:8

I watched as my daddy's eyes were fastened on me and waited to see what the nurses were going to do. He was struggling to breathe on his own. This was not the first time he had faced the enemy of death; as a matter of fact, it was the ninth episode I could remember. We were gathered in the waiting room anticipating another miracle from God. After all, our daddy was only sixty-nine years old.

Suddenly chaos erupted. A beeping alarm sounded, followed by nurses rushing into the room. Surely it was time for Daddy to rally and turn the corner the way he had all those other times!

As the beeping alarm continued, I cried in a loud voice, "Daddy, look at me!" I quoted God's promises with a firm voice as I walked from one side of the bed to the other. I waved my hands, praying, "In the name of Jesus, I pray that you will be healed, Leon Vernon, in the name of Jesus!" Fervently I cried with every ounce of faith—the faith my dad had helped nurture since I was a young girl. Fearlessly and unwaveringly I recalled and recited the Word of God from years of Bible study and Scripture memorization.

Daddy had prompted my three sisters and me to stop reciting the repetitive adolescent prayer at the dinner table when I was nine years old. He encouraged us to pray our own joyful prayers of thanksgiving. Now as I stood in his room in the intensive care unit, I prayed the triumphant words he had taught me, anticipating the Great Physician's healing touch. It was my turn to bolster his faith with prayers of intercession.

I did not have to search for words that had been written by a poet or a writer. I poured out my heart to the Lord, interceding for my dad. I called on all the scriptures and promises from a lifetime of lessons. My faith was strong. I felt certain God would touch Daddy one more time.

I marched back and forth in that room, interceding for my preacher daddy. I just knew we were going to win. We had prayed all those other times in faith, and God had moved mountains. We fervently believed that God would give us another great miracle.

We continued praying throughout that long day and into the evening. Hour after hour we prayed and interceded, our faith never wavering. But it became apparent that this time was different. Regardless of our prayers and intercession and the skill of the doctors and medical personnel, that was the day our Heavenly Father called Daddy home.

As we stood there by his bedside, we watched him pass from death unto life. I thought, *What happened to my miracle?* I had been so convinced God would heal Daddy.

As that long, dark night drifted into the early light of dawn, I began to realize that God *had* performed a miracle. Daddy had experienced the ultimate healing! Underlying our heartache, loss, and grief, the deep certainty that Daddy was experiencing all he had taught and preached throughout his life began swelling within each of us. Daddy was in the presence of Jesus!

I began to finally understand what had happened to my miracle. God had chosen to totally restore Daddy by taking him home. Finally his body was perfect. My dad was personally experiencing everything he preached about and anticipated all his life. I was comforted by God's promises of heaven as words and scriptures flooded my thoughts.

Although I'm still deeply saddened by the loss of my daddy and miss him so much, I'm at peace. God didn't answer my prayer the way I thought He would, but I have a sweet assurance that He's still in control. Although God took my precious father home instead of choosing to heal him, my faith has never wavered.

Maybe that's the greatest miracle of all.

PRAYER: *Heavenly Father, may we always be grateful for your miracles—even when they may not be the ones we had hoped for.*

THOUGHT FOR THE DAY: Heaven will be the perfection we have always longed for. It will be filled with health, vigor, virility, knowledge, happiness, worship, love, and perfection (Billy Graham).

# THE EXIT ROW
## JOYCE WILLIAMS

*You will be my witnesses*
—Acts 1:8

Nothing steps up our Christian witness like a brush with mortality.

"We have an emergency! Our plane is been diverted." My attention was riveted on the flight attendant's urgent whisper as she leaned over my seat in the exit row. My heart was pounding as my mind raced. "You realize you're seated in the exit row. Are you prepared to work with me? You must realize that the lives of the other passengers may be in your hands. Are you okay with this?"

"I'm okay," I answered. Frankly, I was glad to be by that door. I watched carefully as she demonstrated the evacuation procedure. After she hurried back down the aisle, I pulled out the card from the seatback in front of me and intently reviewed the procedures. Then I prayed for a safe landing.

Just a few moments later, the pilot announced the cause of our imminent emergency—a problem with the landing gear. He told us we were being diverted to National Airport in Washington, D.C. He tried to reassure us, saying that every possible precaution would be taken. Startled passengers looked at each other in consternation. Eleven executives from the same corporation began discussing possible ramifications if they did not survive.

As I prayed, the Lord ministered to me, saying, *In the same way that you're the doorkeeper to safety on this plane, as a believer you're a gatekeeper to life everlasting. My people are always seated on the exit row. You know the way of escape. My followers are the channels through which I've chosen to spread the good news!*

Fifteen minutes later, we were told to brace for landing. Glancing out my window, I saw the blinking red lights of emergency vehicles. We all got into the emergency landing position. Those moments of approach and touchdown—a much-too-gentle term—were agonizing. Skillfully, the pilot maneuvered the plane to a grinding halt. Immediately the doors were opened, and we hurriedly exited down makeshift steps and were directed to a waiting van that whisked us off to the terminal.

Airline officials met with the passengers, and then we boarded a bus to our original destination, Roanoke, Virginia, my hometown. I've always enjoyed sharing my faith, but that prompting of the Holy Spirit heightened my awareness of the need to share my faith.

On that four-hour bus journey, it was a great privilege to engage in conversation with my fellow travelers. They readily responded to my gentle questions about their faith. I was blessed to tell them about Jesus and hand out cards that I always carry with me that explain the plan of salvation.

Some had questions; others talked about attending church as a child. One was a committed Christian. I prayed that the Lord would use this interaction for His glory to turn hearts toward Him.

A week later, my husband, Gene, and I flew back to Washington, D.C., for a meeting. That evening we encountered a long line at a restaurant near our hotel, so we took the pager they gave us to alert us when our table was ready and went outside to wait. A man graciously offered to share his bench with us.

As we waited, Gene and I introduced ourselves and exchanged pleasantries with the gentleman, whose name was Will. When he learned that my husband is a minister, he began asking poignant questions about God. Gene patiently responded to each question. Then it dawned on me—we were seated in Will's eternal exit row!

About that time our pager buzzed—the first time it was ever too early! As Gene went inside to secure our table, I told him I would be right there. Will had more questions. Finally, I said, "Why don't you join us for dinner?" So Will joined us, and our discussion continued.

Over dessert, Will began to weep. "I'm desperate to experience God as you know Him!" I pulled out one of those little cards I always carry and told him the miraculous news of Jesus' provision for our salvation. Eagerly he prayed with Gene to accept Christ—right there in the restaurant. We rejoiced with him and exchanged contact information so we could send resources and stay in touch.

Gene and I practically floated back to our hotel that night. Our hearts were full of thanksgiving that our "exit row bench" had led to the ultimate escape.

PRAYER: *Thank you, Father, for divine encounters that change lives for eternity.*

THOUGHT FOR THE DAY: We never know when the eternal lives of others will be in our hands.

# LESSON WITH A HAIRBRUSH

## BETH MOORE

*The King will reply, "I tell you the truth, whatever you did for one of these least of these brothers of mine, you did for me."*
—Matthew 25:40

I was heading to the East Coast, and I had a layover in Knoxville, Tennessee. I was going from a rather large airplane to a very small plane, so I joined other travelers in one large room with several doors leading to commuter aircraft. Wanting to make good use of an hour layover, I sat with my Bible on my lap and continued to work on memorizing the first chapter of John.

Incidentally, I know no better way to memorize scripture than on an airplane. If you can't memorize well, you need to fly. You just read a small portion of scripture out loud a number of times and then look out the window of the plane and try to say it from memory. I don't know why it works so well. Perhaps being up in the air is more conducive to higher thoughts. You'll have to try it for yourself.

I'll warn you, however: you may or may not prove a blessing to the person sitting next to you. At one point on the plane ride to Knoxville, I got stumped on the next word, and the woman sitting next to me filled it in for me. And she didn't appear blessed.

Back to the layover. I had the Bible on my lap and was very intent upon what I was doing. I had had a marvelous morning with the Lord. I say that because I want to tell you that sometimes it's a scary thing to have the Spirit of God really working in you. You could end up doing some things you never would have done otherwise. Life in the Spirit can be dangerous for a thousand reasons, not the least of which is your ego.

Seventy or eighty of us filled this commuter area of the Knoxville airport, all waiting to board our planes. The seating in this large room had us facing one another in various rows of vinyl chairs. I see that particular arrangement often in airports, but I've never been able to figure it out. Certainly I'm a people-watcher, but I prefer to do my people-watching a little less conspicuously.

All at once the people sitting across from me were captivated by a sight over my shoulder. I smoothed down my hair, thinking my Texas-do might have been a bit much for them. In Texas we tend to believe the higher the hair, the closer to God, but I've noticed that other regions in the nation may not have reached such deep revelation.

Since their expressions didn't change after I calmed my hair into submission, I knew something was going on behind my back. From the look of their expressions, I could also tell it was horrifying. I wanted to look so badly, but Southern girls who mind their manners know you don't stare while everyone else is staring. You wait to stare until all the others have stopped.

I tried as hard as I could to keep my eyes on my Bible, but I was so distracted by my fellow travelers that I couldn't concentrate. I had no idea what was going on back there, but I knew it had to be something big. In just a few minutes I could see activity over my left shoulder, and finally I glanced out of the corner of my eye. I'll never forget what I saw: an airline attendant was pushing a wheelchair with an old man who looked not a day younger than 127 years old.

I've never in my whole life seen a human being look that old and that weary and that drawn. I tried to keep from staring, but he was such a strange sight. Humped over in a wheelchair, he was skin and bones dressed in clothes that obviously fit when he was at least twenty pounds heavier. His knees protruded from his trousers, and his shoulders looked as if the coat hanger were still in his shirt. His hands looked like tangled masses of veins and bones. The strangest part of him was his hair and nails. Stringy grey hair hung well over his shoulders and down part of his back. His fingernails were long and clean. They were unpainted, thankfully, but strangely out of place on such an old man.

I looked back down at my Bible as fast as I could, discomfort burning my face. As I tried to imagine what his story might have been, I found myself wondering if I had just had a Howard Hughes sighting. Then again, I had read somewhere that he was dead. So this man in the airport—an impersonator maybe? Was a camera on us somewhere? I recall being on an airplane on my way to Memphis once with a planeful of Elvis impersonators. Unbeknownst to me, it was the king of rock and roll's birthday. I had never seen so many men with bigger hair than mine or such a penchant for talking in lyrics. Okay, don't be cruel. The point is, the strange old man could have been an act, I supposed. But if he was, he deserved an Oscar—and a new makeup artist.

There I sat trying to concentrate on the Word to keep from being concerned about a thin slice of humanity served on a wheelchair only a few seats from me. All the while, my heart was growing more and more overwhelmed with feeling toward him. Let's admit it. Curiosity is a heap more comfortable than true concern, and suddenly I was awash with aching emotion for this bizarre-looking old man.

I had walked with God long enough to see the handwriting on the wall. I've learned that when I begin to feel what God feels, something so contrary to my natural feelings, something dramatic is bound to happen. And it may be embarrassing. I immediately began to resist, because I could feel God working on my spirit and moving me toward the man. I started arguing with God in my mind. *Oh, no, God—please, no.* I looked up at the ceiling as if I could stare straight through it into heaven and said silently, *Please, Lord—I know what's going on here. You want me to witness to this man. Not right here and now. Please! I'll do anything. Put me on the same plane, but don't make me get up here and witness to this man in front of this gawking audience. Please, Lord!*

Don't get me wrong, I don't have a problem with sharing the gospel with someone. I love to share Jesus, but this was a very peculiar-looking man in a setting that seemed a bit non-conducive to spiritual awakening. I tried my hardest to continue my memory work when I felt a serious rebuke from God—something like "Hide my Word in your heart. Don't hide in my Word *from* your heart." His Word is meant to teach us how to love Him and love others. To use the study of God's Word as an excuse not to serve is like using food as an excuse not to eat.

Then I heard His commanding voice loud and clear. When I say God spoke to me, it wasn't an audible voice. Like most of you, I would have instantly morphed into a corpse. Rather, a very clear statement entered my mind that I knew wasn't my own thought or imagination. In my experience, I usually know God is speaking by three conditions.

First of all, what I believe I "heard" has to be consistent with His Word. God never speaks contrary to Scripture. The character of God expressed in the whole counsel of His Word is how we know, for instance, that God never tells mothers to kill their children no matter how a tormented woman may insist He has.

Second, what I believe I "heard" sometimes seems to come somewhere out of left field, and I know I wasn't even on the same intellectual track at that moment. In other words, it wasn't me, and it was consistent with God.

Third, I'm far more likely to discern the voice of God accurately if I'm in the Spirit. I don't mean something mystical by being "in the Spirit." I'm talking about being in close fellowship with God and the fruit of the Spirit infiltrating my own. When I'm in a spiritual condition to really listen, and He's speaking something clearly consistent with His Word but quite different from my own thoughts, I usually think, *That's got to be God.* Sometimes I'm off base. This wasn't one of those times.

There I sat in the blue vinyl chair begging His Highness, *Please don't make me witness to this man. Lord, please, please! Not now! I'll do it on the plane if you'll put us on the same plane.*

Then I heard it: *Oh, I don't want you to witness to him—I want you to brush his hair.*

The words were so clear, my heart leapt into my throat, and my thoughts spun like a top. My chin practically dropped to the ground with shock as I quickly surveyed the two prospects. Do I witness to the man or brush his hair? A no-brainer. I looked straight up to the ceiling and said, *God, as I live and breathe, I want you to know that I'm ready to witness to this man. I'm on this, Lord. I'm your girl! You've never seen a woman witness to a man faster in your life! What difference does it make if his hair is a mess if he's not redeemed? I'm on him. I'm going to witness to this man!*

Again, as clearly as I've ever heard an audible word, God seemed to write this statement across the wall of my mind: *That's not what I said, Beth. I don't want you to witness to him. I want you to go brush his hair.*

I looked up at God and quipped, *I don't have a hairbrush. It's in my suitcase on the plane, for crying out loud! How am I supposed to brush his hair without a hairbrush?* Where I come from, you fix your hair, spray it stiff, and don't touch it again until bedtime. Clearly this wasn't bedtime. God was so insistent that I almost involuntarily began walking toward the man as these thoughts came to me from God's Word: "[I will] thoroughly [furnish you] unto all good works" (1 Timothy 3:7, KJV) I stumbled over to the wheelchair, thinking I could use one myself. Even as I retell this story to you, my pulse has quickened, and I can feel those same butterflies. I knelt down in front of the man and asked as demurely as possible, "Sir, may I have the pleasure of brushing your hair?"

He looked back up at me and said, "What'd you say?"

"May I have the pleasure of brushing your hair?"—to which he responded in volume ten, "Little lady, if you expect me to hear you, you're going to have to talk louder than that."

At this point I took a deep breath and blurted out, "SIR," (no, I'm not exaggerating) "MAY I HAVE THE PLEASURE OF BRUSHING YOUR HAIR?" At that point every eye in the place darted right at me. I was the only thing in the room more peculiar than old Mr. Longlocks. Face crimson and forehead breaking out in a sweat, I watched him look up at me with absolute shock on his face and say, "If you really want to."

Are you kidding? Of course I didn't want to! But God didn't seem interested in my personal preferences right about then. He pressed on my heart until I could utter the words, "Yes, sir, I would be so pleased. But I have one little problem. I don't have a hairbrush."

"I have one in my bag," he responded. I went around the back of that wheelchair, and I got down on my hands and knees. I unzipped the stranger's old carry-on, hardly believing what I was doing. I lifted out undershirts, pajamas, and shorts until I finally came to the bottom of the bag. There my fingers wrapped around the familiar bristles of a brush. I stood up and started brushing the old man's hair. It was perfectly clean, but it was tangled and matted. I don't do many things well, but I must admit I've had notable experience untangling knotted hair, mothering two little girls.

As I had done with either Amanda or Melissa in such a condition, I began brushing at the bottom of the strands, remembering to take my time and be careful not to pull.

A miraculous thing happened to me as I started brushing that old man's hair. Everybody else in the room disappeared. There was no one alive for those moments except that old man and me. I brushed and I brushed and I brushed until every tangle was out of that hair. I know this sounds so strange, but I've never felt that kind of love for another soul in my entire life. I believe with all my heart, I—for that few minutes—felt a portion of the very love of God, that He had overtaken my heart for that little while like someone renting a room and making himself at home for a short while. The emotions were so strong and so pure that I knew they had to be God's.

His hair was finally as soft and smooth as an infant's. I slipped the brush back in the bag and went around the chair to face him. I got down on my knees, put my hands on his knees and said, "Sir, do you know Jesus?"

He said, "Yes, I do." Well, that figures. He explained, "I've known Him since I married my bride. She wouldn't marry me until I got to know the Savior. You see, the problem is, I haven't seen my bride in months. I've had open-heart surgery, and she's been too ill to come see me. I was sitting here thinking to myself, *What a mess I must be for my bride!*"

Only God knows how often He allows us to be part of a divine moment when we're completely unaware of the significance. This, on the other hand, was one of those rare encounters when I knew God had intervened in details only He could have known. It was a God moment, and I'll never forget it.

Our time came to board, and sadly, we were not on the same plane. Oh, how I wished we had been! I was deeply ashamed of how I had acted earlier and would have been so proud and pleased to have accompanied him on that aircraft. The airline attendant came to get him, and we said our good-byes, and she rolled him onto the plane.

I said, "Do you know Jesus? He can be the bossiest thing!" And we got to share. I learned something about God that day I'll never forget. He knows if you're exhausted because you're hungry, you're serving in the wrong place, or it's time to move on but you feel too responsible to budge. He knows if you're hurting or feeling rejected. He knows if you're sick or drowning under a wave of temptation. Or He knows if you just need your hair brushed. God knows your need. He sees you as an individual. Tell Him your need.

I got onto my own flight, sobs choking my throat, wondering how many opportunities just like that one I had missed along the way—all because I didn't want people to think I was strange. God didn't send me to that old man—He sent that old man to me.

PRAYER: *Father, may I always obey your still, small voice.*

THOUGHT FOR THE DAY: Only God knows how often He allows us to be part of a divine moment when we're completely unaware of the significance (Beth Moore).

In stripes, in imprisonments, in tumults, in labors (2 Corinthians 6:5)—in all these things, display in your life a drawing on the grace of God, which will show evidence to yourself and to others that you are a miracle of His. Draw on grace now, not later. The primary word in the spiritual vocabulary is *now*. Let circumstances take you where they will, but keep drawing on the grace of God in whatever condition you may find yourself (Oswald Chambers, *My Utmost for His Highest,* June 26).

———•———

# IN A MOST UNLIKELY PLACE

## LARRY PAGE

*Since God chose you to be the holy people whom he loves, you must clothe yourselves with tenderhearted mercy, kindness, humility, gentleness and patience. You must make allowance for each other's faults and forgive the person who offends you. Remember, the Lord forgave you, so you must forgive others. And the most importance piece of clothing you must wear is love. Love is what binds us all together in perfect harmony. And let the peace that comes from Christ rule in your hearts.*
—Colossians 3:12-15, NLT

One of the things I love most about being a youth pastor is taking our teens on mission trips. I really believe we learn far more from these experiences than do the ones we have gone to teach. Such was the case with James Alvarez. We were deeply touched by his testimony.

James cringed with horror as five evil gamblers restrained him, forcing his father and him to watch as they brutally attacked his mother. They raped her repeatedly, beat her, and then ruthlessly murdered her. Even though James was just a child, they turned on him, beating him and leaving him for dead.

Although his father was a pastor, he loved the world more than he loved God. James was deeply distressed when Papa started gambling. That night James's mother died, the five shady characters had gotten together to hustle James's father. They let him win several games, and then they started winning their money back. They told his father, "We like your wife. If you win this hand, we will give you all the money and walk away. But if we win, we get to have our way with her." James was horrified when his dad agreed. And then his dad lost.

James survived, barely. He spent six months in a coma. Several Christian friends visited him faithfully, praying for him. They talked to him, although he couldn't respond. The doctors believed he was brain dead, so they invited medical students to come to learn and watch as they cut on his body. They were going to start with his brain. James says he still remembers the lights of the hallway going by as he was rolled along on the table.

As he lay there in the morgue, he heard the surgical saw they would use to cut into his scalp getting closer. Screaming silently, he cried, *God—I'm not dead! Please give me one chance and rescue me! I promise I'll serve you the rest of my life!*

In that moment his hand reached up and grabbed the arm of the doctor who was holding the saw. Speaking for the first time in six months, he cried out, "I am not dead!" Astonished, the doctor turned off the saw. Later, he and two nurses gave their lives to Christ. James kept praying over and over, *Thank you, God. I am alive!*

As he recovered, the police questioned him. He had no choice but to tell them about his father as well as the men who had attacked him and killed his mother. His father was imprisoned and ended up dying there. But James visited his father in prison and told him about Jesus. He told him that in spite of all he had done to hurt his family, he forgave him.

James lived in several orphanages. He went to school when he could. In his early twenties he married, and he and his wife had a daughter named Angel. But it wasn't long until his wife decided she wanted to be with another man who could give her more things. She left James to care for little Angel. Angel accepted the Lord as her Savior and had strong faith. A few years later, James married a woman named Lupita, whose daughter, Juanita, was the same age as Angel.

When she was fourteen, Angel became very sick, and the doctors couldn't determine what was wrong with her. She was in constant pain. After months of watching her suffer, James felt he could hardly bear it any longer. While praying one day, he told the Lord, *If you choose to heal my sweet Angel, then please touch her. But if you don't, it's okay. I will always love you, Lord. You are my God and my Savior. If she is not going to get better, then please take her to be with you so she won't suffer any longer.* A few days later, Angel went to be with the Lord. James grieved for his Angel, but he had great peace knowing she was no longer in pain.

James remained strong, loving Lupita and Juanita very much. Although neither of them has accepted Jesus as their Savior, he continues praying for them. Juanita thinks James doesn't know that she sneaks his Bible into their room, locks the door, and reads it. That makes him smile.

Both Juanita and Lupita have witnessed many occasions when James's faith has shown that God is real and in control of his life. Since they're very poor, they usually eat only one meal a day. One day there was no food in the refrigerator or their tiny pantry. As James was reading his Bible and praying, God told him, *Trust me. I will provide everything you need.*

In the kitchen Juanita was crying, saying, "I really want some chicken. I'm so hungry! I wish we had some chicken to eat."

Lupita replied, "Don't you understand? There's nothing here at all, and yet you want chicken."

Juanita said, "Please tell Papa James I want some chicken."

"Can't you see how sad he is because he can't provide something for us to eat? Lupita said. "There is no work. There is no money. Yet you want to beg him to get chicken. You can't do that!"

But Lupita asked him anyway. Then she said, "Please pray to your God to help us have some food to eat."

James replied, "Somehow the Lord will provide just what we need."

A while later James got a call from his brother and his wife. They wanted to come to dinner and bring their three children. So by faith, James replied, "Sure! Come and have dinner." James waited a few minutes. Then he told Lupita.

She became very angry, crying out, "We have no money and no food for ourselves, but you invite your family? Are you loco?"

James said, "Don't worry. God is in control, and He will provide."

Throughout the afternoon James continued praying and checking with people about work and money. There was nothing. At dinnertime his brother and family arrived. James went out to greet them and said, "Brother, I am so sorry. I told you to come to dinner, and we have absolutely nothing to offer you to eat. I am so embarrassed."

His brother put his arm around James' shoulder and said, "Don't worry, brother. You misunderstood our phone conversation. We have brought plenty of food. There will be some extra left over to leave for you and your family."

As they went to get the food from the car, his brother turned to James and said, "I hope you don't mind, but we went ahead and picked up two buckets of Kentucky Fried Chicken for tonight."

Tears swelled in James' eyes as he breathed a prayer of thanks. That night they celebrated as they feasted on an abundance of delicious food. As they licked their fingers, they rejoiced together, thanking God for His provision.

Although James continues facing many challenges, his faith remains strong. He truly comprehends that forgiveness is always part of God's plan. To be honest, as James explained what had happened to his mother and what his father had done, I started to get angry for him. But his response was "If I hadn't forgiven my papa for what he did, I would be no better than he was. I am sad to this day about all that happened. But who am I to harbor an unforgiving spirit in my heart after all the Lord has forgiven and done for me?"

He went on to say, "Some days I feel very lonely and wish I had my family around to share my life. My mama, papa, and daughter—all of them are gone. But, praise God, I have Jesus, and the Holy Spirit is right here with me. So I am okay. My life has never been the same since I asked God to take over that day on the hospital gurney. Even when God allows tough things to come into our lives, He always knows what is best. We just need to trust and obey Him."

The last day we were there, after we finished working, James was alone in the tool shed rearranging things. As I walked by, I heard him singing the words of a well-known hymn: "Trust and obey, for there's no other way to be happy in Jesus but to trust and obey."

To this day, I thank God for allowing our paths to cross. Despite his tremendous hardships, James is a model of Christlike forgiveness. When we trust Him and obey Him, God is with us, even when things don't turn out the way we wish they would. Our Heavenly Father never forsakes us—even in life's darkest moments.

PRAYER: *Dear Father, please enable me to forgive as I have been forgiven.*

THOUGHT FOR THE DAY: God turns our tests into testimonies.

# THE JEEP

## GARY PARRISH

*You will not fear the terror of night.*
—Psalm 91:5

My heart was deeply moved when I heard about the devastation caused by Hurricane Katrina. When the desperate call went out for volunteer doctors and medical personnel, I knew I must go to New Orleans. Since I am an emergency room physician, my schedule was flexible, so I quickly made arrangements to head south. Before long I was working in an emergency room—all by myself. I spent a week working there, and my heart ached for those dear people. Ninety-five per cent of the patients I treated had lost everything.

On Thursday I worked until two o'clock in the afternoon. Then I climbed into my Jeep for the six-hour drive back to Ft. Walton Beach, Florida, I was scheduled on a 5:15 A.M. flight from Pensacola the next morning that would allow me to get home to Roanoke, Virginia, in time for my shift in the emergency room there. My Jeep was packed with medicine and supplies.

All the rest areas had been destroyed by the hurricane. I inched along on the one-lane interstates and finally crossed into Alabama at dusk. Suddenly the Jeep began making a strange, thumping noise, so I pulled into the Alabama Welcome Center. To my dismay, I discovered that I had a flat tire. I called AAA, and the tow truck arrived more than an hour later.

I called my sister, Brenda, in Nashville to let her know what was going on. Then I called the airline and changed my flight to a noon departure the next day. However, it didn't take the tow truck driver long to realize that his tools would not work for my Jeep. To complicate matters further, his truck broke down as well. By this time it was 9:30 P.M.

He finally got his truck going and towed me to Mobile, Alabama. We checked with several motels, but there were no rooms available. I asked the driver to tow my vehicle to a Firestone store. I knew they opened early, and I could get my new tire and then head for the airport.

I reached for my cell phone to call Brenda. To my consternation, as I anxiously patted my pockets and searched the Jeep, I realized that I must have left my phone on the bench at the rest area. There I was—marooned in the Firestone parking lot with no place to spend the night. I had no operational vehicle, and it was not the safest part of town. Although I had money in my pocket and credit cards in my wallet, I felt homeless and abandoned—as some of the hurricane victims with whom I had been working must have felt. I whispered prayers and finally went to sleep sitting in the front seat of the Jeep. As I drifted off, I could almost hear God respond, *You're going to get through this. I'm in charge here!*

I was fast asleep at 2:00 A.M. when I was abruptly awakened by a knock on my window. My heart was pounding when I saw two guys and one girl. I thought, *This is it! I'm dead.*

To my amazement, the girl said, "Gary, we know who you are." *How could she know my name?* Then she went on to say, "Don't be afraid. We found your cell phone at the rest area and decided to call your numbers to see if we could find out whose phone this is. We reached Brenda and talked to her for a long time. She told us what you had been doing and about your predicament. So we called AAA. Then we finally reached the tow truck driver, who told us where you were."

They went on to explain that one of the guys was in the military and on a forty-eight-hour leave. He and his cousins had been headed to Pensacola before their detour to find me.

After talking to Brenda, they looked at each other and said, "We're going to get Gary!" They turned around and drove back seventy-three miles to my exit. They followed the tow truck driver's directions and found my Jeep in the Firestone lot. Then they handed over my cell phone.

The young people waited with me until the store opened. I made arrangements for the tire to be replaced and told them I would pick up the Jeep when I returned to Florida in a couple of weeks. Then my "angels of mercy" drove me to Pensacola so I was able to catch the noon flight.

The young woman called Brenda the next day to make sure I got home okay. Later, when I talked to her and said I wanted to send a check to reimburse them, she immediately responded, "Don't spoil this by sending money to us." She went on to say, "By the way, my husband is a tow truck driver. That's how we were able to find out who had towed you."

PRAYER: *Father, may we always trust you. Help me remember that even in the dark times of my life, I'm never alone. Thank you that your promises outshine the blackest night.*

THOUGHT FOR THE DAY: When you are in the dark, listen, and God will give you a very precious message for someone else once you are back in the light (Oswald Chambers).

# MARKS OF GRACE
## KIM POUND

*[He] healed those who needed healing.*
—Luke 9:11

On January 19, 2008, miracles starting raining down from heaven upon our family. It was a strange way for miracles to begin, however, because they started when my husband, Darin, was seriously injured in a boating accident. By all accounts the doctors say Darin is fortunate to be alive, but I know he was spared by the grace of our miracle-working Heavenly Father.

It had been a great day on the water near our home in Homestead, Florida. Darin had taken our children and a missionary friend for a ride in our boat.

Suddenly everything went wrong. The boat lurched, and Darin was thrown overboard into the boat's trim tab and critically injured. The inside of his left arm was cut from between his little finger and ring finger almost to the crease of his elbow—a long, deep 12-inch cut. Several bones in his wrist were broken, his other bones in his arm were shattered, all the tendons were severed, and an artery in his hand was nicked. His arm had been laid wide open, and blood gushed from his wounds.

God's hand was apparent immediately. The accident occurred eight miles from shore. There was no ladder on our boat, but with God's help, Darin was able to get back into the boat. Other boaters nearby found someone to drive our boat in, as well as a towboat to lead the way.

Someone was supposed to have called 911, but the dispatcher from the towboat felt impressed to call himself. We are so thankful he did, because we learned later there had been no earlier call about the accident. When they got into the channel, the Coast Guard was just leaving to come and help. If they had not been there when they were, Darin might have bled to death. The ambulance and airlift crew were waiting when they got to the marina.

While medical personnel worked on Darin, a family nearby was backing their boat into the water. They had three small children buckled into the back seat. For some reason the truck went into the water with the boat. Because of Darin's accident and the emergency personnel on hand, all three children were rescued unharmed. Darin later said that if his accident happened for no other reason than to save those children, it was worth it. It has been so hard to watch Darin's suffering, but as the mother of our own three children, I understand.

Darin was airlifted to Jackson Memorial Hospital in Miami. They called me to pick up our girls and friends from the marina. At that time, as far as I knew, Darin needed just "a few stitches." He had instructed them not to alarm me. When I found out how badly he was injured, it seemed as if my world was moving in slow motion.

It was cold and dreary outside as I raced into the ER. Darin was a pastor, and he and I had been there many times before to be with others from our church. That day, Darin and I were the ones needing care. When I walked through the double doors I looked into the room on my left. I could see that it had been used for a trauma. I wondered if it had been Darin's room. I could hardly breathe.

I heard my name called from the nurse's station. The nurse told me I needed to sign some paperwork in order to get Darin's personal belongings. He put a clear bag in front of me containing Darin's blood-stained clothes. There was also a tiny bag with Darin's blood-stained wedding ring in it. From that moment on I don't remember much of what was said to me.

I followed the nurse into a cubicle, and he pulled back the curtain. My Darin was there! He was alive! I felt a rush of relief, and I could breathe again. Darin was my miracle.

Darin underwent surgery that night to clean the wound and stabilize his arm. He had another surgical procedure a few days later to clean the wound again to guard against infection.

God continued to walk with us. We were told it was miraculous that there was no infection because the accident happened in the ocean. The doctor said Darin was fortunate that only a minor artery was nicked.

She went on to tell us that before they could do his third surgery, the bones would need to heal enough for her to be able to insert a long metal plate in his arm and secure it. Pins would need to be placed in his wrist as well.

Our church was having revival in February with Gene Williams as our guest speaker. Darin was supposed to remain at home resting—staying away from people to safeguard against infection because the wound was still open. But he wanted to go to church, so on Sunday night we went late and sat in the back. Gene was at the altar, praying with people for healing.

When he finished praying, Darin spoke up and asked if he had time for one more. As Gene prayed for Darin, he asked God to touch him. He prayed, "Let the doctors be amazed and say his bones are healed." Then Darin and the girls and I went home because he was still quite weak.

We realized the following week when Darin had surgery just how important that prayer was. He was in the operating room a long time. But when the surgeon came out, I remembered Gene's prayer—because the surgeon said, "I am amazed! The bones were healed enough to secure the plate, and the wrist bones were healed as well; we did not have to put pins in them!" She went on to tell Darin that he was an amazingly quick healer. We rejoiced at her words. I wish we had told her who the partner in healing had been.

Darin had one more surgery for a skin graft. It was not immediately successful, but it healed in God's timing. He had physical therapy for several months. It was a painful process, but well worth the work.

Today Darin is able to use his arm and hand. He can write again, and he is now able to make and hold a fist. He is still working on his range of motion. God continues to work in our lives.

The Lord had been speaking to us about leaving our comfortable, wonderful ministry at our church in Redland, Florida, to go to Belize as volunteer missionaries. On Palm Sunday, just two months to the day after Darin's accident, the Lord led Darin to resign as senior pastor of our church. By the middle of June—just five months after that terrifying day—we were in Belize! Although the timing may seem strange, we have no doubt that this is God's plan for us.

I have learned through all of this that sometimes miracles come in large sizes, but that the small day-to-day ones are just as important. I look for them because I don't want to miss any.

As our daughter Karissa says, "The scar is Daddy's mark of grace."

PRAYER: *Thank you, Great Physician, for your healing touch and protection on our lives.*

THOUGHT FOR THE DAY: The fingerprints of our Great Physician are all over the lives of those who trust Him (Gene Williams).

# A LIFE REWRITTEN
## AS TOLD TO JOYCE WILLIAMS

*I will put my laws in their minds and write them on their hearts.*
*I will be their God, and they will be my people. . . . For I will*
*forgive their wickedness and remember their sins no more.*
—Hebrews 8:10, 12

I was having lunch with a good friend one day when she said, "Could I tell you my story?" I love it when people do that! I leaned forward and listened intently as she began to share.

He was so handsome, so famous—and that voice! I just couldn't resist going to his quartet's media table following the gospel music concert that night. I could hardly believe it when he seemed to kind of single me out for special attention. I had him autograph his latest album and was really flattered when he continued talking to me.

Then he asked if I would like to get a bite to eat after he finished signing autographs. Somehow I felt like Cinderella at the ball. I don't remember a thing I ate when we met around midnight. I couldn't believe it when he invited me go with him to his room. *Me! Nobody!* Of course, I said yes. Thus began my two-year affair with a married gospel music "star."

I had not grown up in a Christian home. My father was cold and detached, so as a teenager I found myself pursuing the classic pattern of searching for love and acceptance in the wrong places. I was horrified to find I was pregnant at the age of seventeen. Somehow I managed to finish high school.

After my daughter was born I worked two jobs to support us as I steadily enjoyed upward growth in the workplace. Those years were busy and demanding, and I regret that I didn't have more time to spend with my daughter.

In my quieter moments I knew there was a God. Sometimes I even opened a Bible, but I didn't understand anything I read. Then, fourteen years later, I went to that gospel music concert.

I was so confused. After all, I was a nobody, and he was famous. For two years I rationalized the affair. After all, he was the spiritual leader. I loved the music and listened to his songs constantly—singing along with all the lyrics. The words were so full of promise, hope, and joy. I was in love.

As God would have it, the words of some of the songs began to penetrate my rationalizations with His truth. I finally asked God to forgive me for my sins, and for the first time I found genuine joy and peace. I knew I had to end our affair.

I still remember the night I mustered up the courage to tell him it was over. I said, "We can't do this anymore. It's wrong! God has forgiven me. He is calling me out of this lifestyle." He cried. I cried. It was not a pretty scene. But I wouldn't trade anything for the love of God I had finally discovered. I had been forgiven, and miraculously the Lord truly enabled me to forgive.

I later learned that God rocked his world soon afterwards. I had known all along that I was not the only other woman he had been involved with on the gospel concert circuit. I was so grateful for the solid rock of my Savior's pure love for me, and that love held me steady.

That all happened twenty-five years ago. God has rewritten my life with the pen of His limitless mercy and grace. A few years later He led me to a wonderful Christian man. We fell in love and were married. Our lives are centered on our mutual love for God and our church, and our precious teenage daughter is very involved in her youth group. Both my husband and I count it a privilege to be lay leaders in our church.

The Lord has broken the old strongholds on my heart. He keeps me vigilant to guard against things that for so long had a powerful influence on me. I'm thankful to Him for the keen insight He has given me. Many times I've experienced the joy of praying with women who struggle with the same kind of baggage I carried for many years. I still love gospel music, and these days I get to sing at our church.

My friend and I rejoiced as she finished telling me her story. God has not only rewritten her life—He has rewritten her song!

PRAYER: *Thank you, Father, for forgiving the old sins and making all things new through your great grace.*

THOUGHT FOR THE DAY: I will not permit any man to narrow and degrade my soul by making me hate him (Booker T. Washington).

# THROUGH THE EYES OF A CHILD

## BRAD RILEY

*Whatever you did for one of the least of these . . . you did for me.*
—Matthew 25:40

I've always prayed that our children, Corbin and Brooke, would learn to see the divine essence and value of every person they encounter—to be *others-focused*. Regardless of how lowly people may appear to be, they still carry in their persons the image and stamp of God. A good deal of my ministry has been spent working with compassionate outreach projects. My wife, Rhonda, and I have tried to involve our children.

I was so excited when on a warm spring day, in the middle of an upscale neighborhood in San Antonio, my two small children yelled out, "Dad, it looks like someone is living under those trees!"

We had moved to San Antonio from Kansas to pastor a church nestled on thirteen acres of beautiful, peaceful, rolling hills in a wooded area I could see from my office window. I frequently saw deer playing in the meadow.

Focused on driving, I said, "What did you see?"

"It looks like a little hut or something," Corbin said. I pulled into a parking lot, and we walked back to the woods by the church. Little did I know what we were about to encounter—a makeshift, cardboard shanty with an old umbrella for a roof.

I wondered why a homeless person would live in the middle of woods by a busy road in one of the nicer parts of the city. "Let's go see if anyone is in there," I said to the kids. Although we saw scraps of food from someone's garbage and crushed tin cans, no one was there.

As we turned to go, we saw a woman walking toward us. I smiled at her and introduced myself as pastor of the church nearby. She smiled warmly and then shrugged her shoulders, muttering to herself. I finally understood one word—*hungry*. I thought she meant she was hungry. When I heard the word "Budapest," I realized that she was trying to tell us that she was from Hungary.

*Oh, great,* I thought. *She doesn't speak a word of English, and I don't know Hungarian. How could we communicate?* Then I thought *Love is the universal language.* I prayed, *God, please help me communicate that we want to help her.* And He did just that.

The next few months were an amazing time of discovery for our family and the people in our church. We began taking food to Elizabeth's hut and ultimately moved her into a room in our church. We found Julia, a Jewish lady from Armenia, who translated for us.

Elizabeth slowly began to comprehend that we wanted to help her. She told us she wanted to return to Hungary. It was such a blessing to watch God's love manifested through that group of Christians who worked selflessly to help a homeless foreigner.

A couple of doctors in our church made sure Elizabeth received the medical attention she needed. We learned that she had undergone heart valve replacement surgery a few years earlier and had not had her blood thinner medicine in a long time. Rhonda and the kids went shopping to buy new clothes for her. Our people started a fund to help send Elizabeth back to Hungary and to give her a new start when she get home.

We finally discovered that Elizabeth had come to America about a year earlier to care for her daughter who lived nearby. Sadly, her daughter had experienced a nervous breakdown with serious mental health complications. She had come to America to get away from the old country and resented Elizabeth for following her. After a few months, she threw Elizabeth out. She destroyed her return ticket and records, leaving Elizabeth destitute in the city—in the country illegally since her visa had expired.

By May our people had raised enough money to send Elizabeth back to Hungary and give her a new start in life. Although we would have loved to keep her, she wanted to go home. We helped her with the necessary paperwork and bought the plane tickets. Our family drove her to the airport in Dallas.

We helped her get checked in. As we left the airport, we were all crying. We would miss Elizabeth. I thanked God for sending her to us—to our family and to the church. She was a gift from God—an opportunity to unconditionally love someone in great need. She gave us the chance to put Jesus' words into practice as we fed someone who was truly hungry, clothed someone who had only the shirt on her back, and visited someone in the lonely prison of being alone in a foreign land.

As we drove home, we wondered how many other Elizabeths are out there living under bridges or in the woods. Corbin and Brooke agreed that it felt good to help someone in need. They were both so glad we had found Elizabeth.

I call Elizabeth in Hungary occasionally to say the few words of English that she knows, "I love you, and Jesus loves you too." She is grateful for the miracle of God's love that was poured over her through the people in our church. I am glad that Corbin and Brooke were part of being God's hand extended to bring hope and love to a homeless woman far from home—memories they will carry for a lifetime.

PRAYER: *Father, may we always see others through your eyes of love and compassion.*

THOUGHT FOR THE DAY: It is our care for the helpless, our practice of lovingkindness that brands us. "Look!" they say, "how they love one another" (Tertullian).

# FREEDOM IN
# THE STORM

## DANA ROBERTS

*The storm subsided, and all was calm.*
—Luke 8:24

There we sat, huddled together with our noses pressed against the living room windows, watching our neighbor's big oak tree sway ominously. Every twenty minutes or so we would hurry back to the television set to watch the latest developments on Hurricane Ike. Then we would begin the conversation again: "What do you think? Should we stay or leave?"

My husband, Kevin, and I had done all we knew to prepare for the destructive storm headed our way. We had stocked up on necessities, moved our outdoor furniture into the garage, pulled potted plants against the house, and prepared the innermost room of our house with bedding, extra clothes, shoes, flashlights, important papers, and cell phones. The generator was moved into the garage for easy access, and we had stocked up on gasoline. We had our lines of communication set and arranged emergency plans with friends in towns north of Houston. In a word, we were hunkered down and waiting.

Even though many ZIP code areas in Harris County were on mandatory evacuation, ours was not. However, some of our neighbors had decided to evacuate anyway, and they encouraged us to do the same. Kevin and I had prayed together and individually about what God wanted us to do. It was plain to see that the weight of our family's safety rested heavily on our shoulders.

At one point, a day or so before Hurricane Ike was scheduled to make landfall, Kevin suggested I take our daughters, Haley and Olivia, to a hotel he had contacted in Dallas. I was adamant that our family not be separated. I knew phone lines would be down, and I couldn't stand the thought of not being able to communicate with Kevin. I remember telling him, "We stand as a family, and we fall as a family." I also remember thinking how scary those words sounded.

We continued to pray. Later in the day, we agreed once and for all that we would ride it out in our home.

Late that night, as the wind began to whistle and the rain began to pound, Kevin called the girls and me into the living room, and we began praying. We prayed for safety for our family and for our home and for wisdom on how to proceed once the hurricane hit. We also reaffirmed for our daughters and for ourselves that God was watching over us. We fully trusted His will. At that point, we were struck with the knowledge that even if we wanted to, we couldn't leave.

That's the moment I experienced freedom. How could I possibly feel so peaceful with a hurricane bearing down on us? I was free from worry about our safety or the house. I was free from fear that one of us would be injured. Even so, we didn't hang out by the windows! I was released from thinking about all the preparations and the to-do list.

And at that moment, I was free from every thought except one. *God, you have guided us, and we have used the common sense you gave us. Now we stand confidently.* I even said to Kevin, "I'm ready. Bring it on!" I kept thinking of a line from a song I had heard several years ago about how sometimes God calms the storm and sometimes He calms His child. That was what was happening to me.

As the winds began howling and the torrential rain slanted sideways, we could see through our tall window that branches were flying through the air. The lightning was tremendous, and it wasn't long until our electricity flickered and went out. Our daughters and our dog were sound asleep in the safe room. I even slept for a couple of hours. Who sleeps when a hurricane is crashing all around?

When the wind and rain were at their worst, I awoke to find Kevin sitting quietly in our front room, keeping watch over the girls and me and our house. I joined him there and watched without fear as the wind and rain howled nonstop for hours. I had a sense of calm and an assurance that we were up to the task of whatever might lie ahead.

I watched with renewed appreciation for the awesomeness of God. Hurricane Ike was five hundred miles wide, yet microscopic to God. I realized again that true freedom comes in the most unexpected ways at the most unexpected times.

Thankfully, we suffered no damage. We were heartbroken for the devastation and heartache Hurricane Ike wrought to so many, including those in our own neighborhood. Our family has done what we could to ease the hardships of others.

On a very personal level, though, I will always remember this hurricane as a time when God graciously and miraculously poured freedom into my life. I pray that it doesn't take another hurricane-sized storm to cause me to rest so fully in Him. I hope I will always remember that when the Son sets us free, we are free indeed—even in the storm.

PRAYER: *Thank you, Father, for giving us peace in the midst of life's storms.*

THOUGHT FOR THE DAY: Anxiety does not empty tomorrow of its sorrows but only empties today of its strength (C. H. Spurgeon).

God's purpose is to enable me to see
that He can walk on the storms
of my life right now
(Oswald Chambers,
*My Utmost for His Highest*).

———•———

# DELIVERED FROM WITCHCRAFT

## KIM SINGSON

*I am the way the truth and the life.*
*No one comes to the Father except through me.*
—John 14:6

He was the village witch doctor. People who were sick or demon-possessed were brought to Lamkhogin Kipgen every day. He "treated" almost two hundred persons each month. Over the years he became widely known in that area of India for his witchcraft and magical powers, which were supposedly passed to him by his father.

He was also a heavy drinker, and many times when he got drunk he beat and tortured his wife and children. Everyone in and around his village was aware of his ruthless hardheartedness.

His wife became a committed Christian who prayed fervently for her husband's salvation. Pastors, evangelists, and missionaries approached him about changing his life, but he simply sneered and turned away. They shook their heads and said, "It's almost as if we're talking to a rock!"

As the years passed, the witch doctor earned fame, power, and money. Thousands of people in and around the state of Manipur in India traveled long distances to come to Lamkhogin, seeking a cure for many diseases.

Very suddenly his son, to whom the witch doctor had been very close, died. It was a difficult blow for that witch doctor. His hard heart was broken.

Since his wife had been a member of our church for some time, the family asked me to preach the funeral service. I prayed fervently, seeking God's guidance. I wanted to be sure the Lord enabled me to make the most of this special opportunity to bring comfort from His Word. I knew this could be God's way of calling all of them to accept Jesus as Lord and Savior.

In the pain of loss and bereavement, Lamkhogin acknowledged that his precious son's death was God's way of calling to him. I continued visiting the family to pray with them and also share from God's Word. The local pastor also went by frequently to talk with them about Jesus and to pray with them.

Nothing seemed to work, though. Lamkhogin continued with his way of life. In spite of all that he had accomplished, though, he had no peace of mind or happiness. Nothing could satisfy him, nor could anything change him.

One day I received the news that Lamkhogin had tried to commit suicide several times. In his most recent attempt, he had drunk poison. He was rushed to the hospital and somehow survived.

Finally Lamkhogin no longer had the strength to ignore the voice of God or resist the call of the Holy Spirit. With the encouragement of his wife, the pastor, and other Christian friends, he began reading the Bible.

Sometime later he shared that as he was reading John 14:1-28, the Lord spoke to his heart. After thirty-two years of involvement in witchcraft, he called out to the one true God. When he prayed the prayer of repentance, God forgave him and changed his heart. He repented of his evil practices and turned toward the Savior. God forgave him for his sins, and his life was transformed.

I was so excited when I was invited to attend the cleansing ceremony of Lamkhogin Kipgen on a Sunday afternoon. All of us there rejoiced as he tore up his magic papers and books and buried them along with other paraphernalia he had used when performing witchcraft.

A miracle has taken place in Lamkhogin's heart. The local church members, the pastor, and all who attended the cleansing ceremony rejoiced and celebrated the wonderful work of God. The family continues to grow together in the Lord.

Lamkhogin has become an ambassador for Christ. He does not hesitate to share the good news of his salvation and tell of the peace and joy the Lord has given him. We've witnessed God's healing touch to overturn the evil powers of darkness. Lamkhogin has been delivered from the darkness of witchcraft to the bright light of God's love and forgiveness.

PRAYER: *Thank you, Father, that there is no darkness that your love cannot penetrate with the light of salvation.*

THOUGHT FOR THE DAY: When asked about the awesome pardon of God's forgiveness, regardless of the depths of our sin and degradation, Gipsy Smith replied, "I've never gotten over the wonder of it all."

# NOT ALONE
## RICK UNDERWOOD

*Be strong in the Lord and in his mighty power. Put on the full armor of God so that you can take your stand against the devil's schemes. For our struggle is not against flesh and blood, but against the rulers, against the authorities, against the powers of this dark world and against the spiritual forces of evil in the heavenly realms. Therefore put on the full armor of God, so when the day of evil comes, you may be able to stand your ground, and after you have done everything, to stand.*
—Ephesians 6:10-13

Following college graduation, I worked as an investigator for a large company for several years. There are many facets to an investigator's job; some are mundane, and some are as exciting as television shows portray. However, detectives agree that surveillance is not the most desirable tactic in the pursuit of prosecutable information. In some cases, eyewitness testimony, video, or photographs are necessary to secure an arrest and conviction. Unlike the popular fifty-two-minute, made-for-TV crime programs, investigations—and especially surveillance—do not go by a script. This was true of one of my most memorable cases.

After viewing available records and connections for an investigation into the theft of hundreds of thousands of dollars in materials, it was determined after consultation with the state attorney's office that in order to prosecute those responsible for the fraud, eyewitness documentation was necessary. The investigation led us to a business in southeast Florida that was located in an urban commercial district.

Our team learned that the illegal activity took between forty-five and ninety seconds to complete. It occurred anytime within a thirty-day period of time. After months of hard work, we were able to narrow the possible timeframe for the commission of the crimes to a ten-day window of opportunity and developed a twenty-four-hour-a-day surveillance plan.

We were aware that the suspects worked together in groups of two to four individuals as lookouts. Our team employed various undercover methods with several different vehicles to blend into the urban commercial alley. We decided to have three investigators in the busy traffic hours of the day and two during the early-morning and late-night hours.

We were in the fourth day of the ten-day surveillance and working twelve-hour shifts to monitor the alley. On that particular morning, as my shift was about to begin, I contacted my partner at 4:15 A.M. I was coordinating our separate arrivals at 4:45 A.M. to relieve our team members, who would appreciate the extra few minutes off. Between our conversation at 4:15 and our arrival time, my partner became very ill and was unable to meet me at the site. Against my better judgment, I declined the offer of the night crew to stay over until the third investigator arrived at eight o'clock that morning.

As the lead investigator on the case, I had been watching the alley for months in order to narrow the window and develop a surveillance plan. I could identify the unique sound of the bread company truck that arrived every morning by 6:30 A.M. I knew when to expect the early-morning cleaning crew. I recognized the homeless men who checked the dumpsters for aluminum cans each morning. I knew that alley well.

At 6:06 I realized things did not feel right. I saw an unfamiliar car make two passes by the alley, and on the third pass it drove into the alley. What we had been waiting for was about to happen, and our plan—my plan—was woefully underdeveloped. Knowing that the men's actions would be completed within ninety seconds, I called for back-up from the sheriff's department and asked God for protection. Then I drove my vehicle over curbs and barriers to approach the men. I expected them to be armed, although I was not.

They did not disappoint. Each of them had a handgun, and semi-automatic weapons were within arm's reach in the open trunk. I announced myself and demanded they put their weapons on the ground and stand against the wall. I looked the larger of the two straight in the eye and said, "Please, please put that gun down, because there are men on the roof of this building and men on the other side of this wall pointing guns at you right now, and I do not want you to be shot!"

Slowly, they set their guns on the ground and put their hands into the air. I stood behind the door of my van, amazed. The record documents that the sheriff's deputies arrived in less than four minutes after my first call and made the arrest. Those were four very long minutes of sanctified filibustering!

A strange thing happened a few hours later when the suspects were interviewed in separate rooms by separate detectives. At the close of the interviews, the two detectives came out and asked me to get the other witnesses ready to interview. I told the detectives that I was aware that I did not use the best judgment, but I was alone in the alley. They said, "You were *not* alone!"

Then they provided identical statements from the suspects stating they were in the alley when a man driving a gray van approached them and told them to stand against the wall. The suspects said there were two men at the south end of the alley with handguns drawn and another officer at the north end of the alley with a shotgun. I repeated to the detectives that I was in the alley alone.

As we debriefed the investigation, I took my share of "What were you thinking?" Everyone involved began calling the investigation "the angel case." The hours of surveillance in this and other cases provided time for many conversations with my partners about family, life, and spiritual issues. They knew that my wife, Donna, and I were youth pastors at our church at the time. We invited them to visit our church, prayed with them, and shared in life's joys and tragedies together.

I'm thankful for God's protection that day and for the avenue He provided for me to witness. It was a joy to share with my partners how God had protected me and how He loves them as much as He loves and cares for my family.

Through the years, when the issues of life with all the joys and challenges come, although in perhaps less tangible and less exciting ways, I've leaned on His promise that I'm never alone. For I've truly witnessed His protection team!

PRAYER: *Thank you, Lord, for surrounding us with your loving watch-care.*

THOUGHT FOR THE DAY: Troubles are often the tools by which God fashions us for better things (Henry Ward Beecher).

# THE LIVING WORD
## KELLY JO VANDERSTELT

*We have this treasure in jars of clay to show that this all-surpassing power is from God and not from us. We are hard pressed on every side, but not crushed; perplexed, but not in despair; persecuted, but not abandoned; struck down, but not destroyed. We always carry around in our body the death of Jesus, so that the life of Jesus may also be revealed in our body.*
—2 Corinthians 4:7-10

One never expects the dreaded phone call that brings earth-shattering news. I was cleaning my kitchen one Saturday when a friend called. "Come to the ball field right away. Curt has been hit in the head with a softball and may need medical attention."

As I headed to the field where the church league was playing, I began praying a desperate plea for God's mercy that was to become my constant prayer for days.

Years earlier at age sixteen, my husband, Curt, had suffered a closed-head injury while playing indoor soccer. Doctors assessed his situation as hopeless. While his father started shopping for a nursing home, God had another plan. In time, Curt relearned everything from walking and talking to reading, writing, and feeding himself. He finished high school, attended college, and married me. I always thought of him as a walking miracle.

A few years later he had another freak knock on the head involving a shoe that came flying off a roller coaster! That resulted in a post-traumatic concussion that required plenty of rest. Head injuries are cumulative.

On the day I got the frightening phone call, the other team had thrown a ball to get Curt out. Instead, the ball had hit him in the back of the head. Curt made it to the base, fell to his knees, and crashed forward, hitting his head—again.

After thirty seconds, he came to and seemed lucid. "Let's get back to the game—I'm fine!" he said. His team insisted that he sit on the bench and put ice on his head. About fifteen minutes later, he became disconnected with his surroundings, so I took him to the emergency room.

A CT scan showed no bleeding or extreme brain swelling, but he was in rapid decline. He was experiencing loss of vision, ringing in his ears, and confusion. His long-term memory was locked up. He knew I was his wife, but he had no memory of our daughter. His short-term memory was no better. Every ten seconds or so he asked me, "What's going on? What are we doing here?" He was upset and suspicious, and his insistent questioning went on and on. This condition of agitation remained unchanged for seventy-seven hours.

Tuesday night, without my knowledge, our church held a prayer vigil. A strong sense of God's peace settled over Curt's hospital room like a blanket, and he calmed down immediately. The next few days brought just baby steps of progress. Bewilderment prevailed. Test upon inconclusive test was done. To make matters worse, Curt developed blood clots in his lungs.

Medical professionals expressed their concern about Curt's lack of progress. The chief neurologist used the dreaded D word—*disability*. I couldn't stomach the taste of that word on my lips. Disabled? My thirty-five-year-old husband? Forgive my lack of objectivity, but my husband is an exceptional person. He is a caring, godly man of integrity. God has given Curt an amazing ability to teach and preach biblical truth in a clear, compelling manner.

*How could this happen to* this *man?* I was incredulous. *God, he is your man. How could this be your plan?* After a career in youth ministry, we had recently moved to northern Wisconsin to restart an ailing church plant. We had been busy getting acclimated and established, weaving our hearts and lives into the fabric of our church and community.

Curt and I were caught up in the momentum of fall planning, ready to burst with enthusiasm about God's work. How could my hardworking husband be taken out of the game at such a crucial point? My stubborn mind couldn't accept such a dire possibility. All I had to fall back on was God's grace and peace. "My ways are higher than your ways," the Holy Spirit reminded my anxious heart.

When we are in the lowest chasms of tragedy, I believe God works through Scripture to touch our broken, petrified souls. He brought to my mind 2 Corinthians 12:9: "My grace is sufficient for you, for my power is made perfect in weakness." He surrounded me with my precious, prayerful church family. People around the globe prayed for Curt.

Doctors told me to prepare for a long road to recovery. Curt's vision and hearing were improving, but unexplained fainting, excruciating headaches, and relentless confusion persisted. The doctors made it clear that his rehabilitation would be a marathon, not a sprint.

On day six, Curt was moved to a rehab hospital. There the intake staff established their goal, which was to help Curt function well enough to live at home again. I was appalled. *My* goal was complete restoration to ministry and life as we had known it! They let me know that I needed to adjust my expectations.

Later the same day, Curt revealed, somewhat conspiratorially, that he had figured out that when people were praying for him, he should close his eyes and be quiet. What a devastating revelation! Curt had a total disconnect from spiritual concepts. He asked me who God was, wanting an explanation. My words didn't seem to sink in at all. As his supper arrived, I headed home. That night was one of the lowest points of my life.

The next day marked one week since the softball hit Curt. My sister, Kristi, and her mother-in-law, Cheri, accompanied me to see him. He did not recognize them. I felt an urging that Curt should hear a promise from Scripture and asked Cheri to read. We chose 1 Peter, since Curt had studied it most recently. As Cheri read, Curt's countenance and demeanor changed before our eyes. Suddenly his expression looked alive. I could tell he wanted to say something.

"By His wounds we are healed. By His wounds we are healed." Curt continued to repeat his paraphrase of 1 Peter 2:24. I was filled with astonishment at his attentiveness. I asked him what he knew about God. Curt replied that God was "the Creator and Sustainer of life, the first Person of the Trinity." These theological words were astounding, coming from a man who didn't know what taking a shower meant the day before.

"What about Jesus?" I quizzed him.

"He is the Second Person of the Trinity, the propitiation for our sins." He went on to quote John 1:1-4.

The three of us sat wiping away tears while Curt couldn't understand what the fuss was all about. He tells people now, "I have no memory of that week at the hospital. It's as if I was taking a long nap and just woke up." Yet we had witnessed the powerful living Word of God work in my husband's brain, restoring his awareness and memory. We felt as if we were in a sacred place.

Curt went on to relay other facts that had previously been missing from his memory. The warmth and brightness of his personality were intact, as well as his celebrated sense of humor.

It was obvious to the therapists, doctors, and nurses that Curt's recovery was abrupt and miraculous. We freely shared with them the story about what happened as we were reading the Bible. They listened, but they were hesitant to own the possibility of a true miracle. They said, "This kind of recovery is highly unusual," and "Congratulations—we never see this!" Be assured—I lived every uncertain moment of that frightening week, and I know that Curt was touched distinctly by God's power.

"That head injury was the best sermon I could have ever preached about prayer," Curt often says, laughing. When he returned to the pulpit, he challenged our congregation to shift all their focused prayer for his recovery to their unsaved friends, neighbors, and co-workers. Since that time, our small, struggling church has tripled in size and has experienced a great rekindling of faith.

And the Word continues to be lived out in our lives.

PRAYER: *Father, I trust you alone to lead me and provide for me in times of joy as well as in days of dark suffering. Thank you for the power and the truth of your living Word.*

THOUGHT FOR THE DAY: If we marinate our hearts in God's Word, the Holy Spirit will bring those living words of comfort to our recollection when storms come into our lives.

# LISTEN FOR
# THE ANGELS

## JOYCE WILLIAMS

*He will command his angels concerning you to guard you in all your ways.*
—Psalm 91:11

My husband, Gene, along with a number of other pastors, has had the privilege of being part of filming nine primetime television specials in Israel and the lands of the Bible. I have been blessed to accompany him on five of those trips. One day when we were getting ready to enter the Catacombs in Rome, I noticed a marble statue of a lovely, reclining teenage girl. When I asked our guide who she was, she related a story that encourages my heart every time I reflect on it.

She said that the beautiful teenager had been arrested along with her family during the intense persecution of the Early Church in Rome. Emperor Nero had ordered that everyone who refused to acknowledge him as god would be tortured and thrown to the hungry lions in the Coliseum. The vicious, gory deaths of those early believers were part of the entertainment for the spectators in the stands evening after evening. Sometimes soldiers were ordered to coat their captives in tar and place them on the stands where the torches stood. Then as twilight fell over the arena, they ignited the tar, and the martyrs became human torches as they burned to death.

When the day came and the soldiers arrived at the prison to take her family away, they told her, "You are so beautiful that we are not going to take you to the lions today. We have plans for you. Emperor Nero might even want you!"

The young girl watched with great sorrow and agony as her family was led away. Imploringly, she reached for her loved ones. But the soldiers had their orders to hold back beautiful young girls, and they restrained her. That evening she could hear the roaring lions and the howling mob as her family died horrifying deaths because of their faith.

Day after day the solders came to her prison cell and said, "All you have to do to be saved from the lions is recant your faith. Just say, 'Nero is god.' It's that simple." Through the agony of her grief for her family, and without ever wavering, she always replied, "I will not do that. Jesus is Lord of my life."

The day finally came when the soldiers said, "This is your last chance. You must acknowledge Nero as god today, or you will be thrown to the hungry lions tonight." To emphasize their point, they said, "Listen. Even now you can hear their roars. You know that they are starving. They will tear you apart. You will die a slow, agonizing death. Don't you remember that we told you how your family died? Just say those simple words, 'Nero is god,' and you will live. You will have a good life." Then one more time they said, "Can't you hear the lions?"

With the glow of her love for Jesus shining in her eyes, she replied, "I will never renounce my faith in Jesus. He is the Lord of my life. Yes. I can hear the lions." Then she paused, and with a radiant smile illuminating her face, she said, "Oh, but can't you almost hear the angels' wings? They are waiting to carry me to Jesus and my family."

True to their words, they angrily grabbed her that evening and carried her off to the Coliseum to her death. That night she was brutally ravaged as the starving lions feasted and the crowd roared.

When our guide finished telling us this story, we looked at the marble statue with new appreciation as we thought of the sacrifice of the early martyrs. Although Nero may have appeared to be the winner that day, the fact remains that this martyr's death was another victory for the Lord. I believe we may one day meet in heaven those who came to know Jesus because of her martyrdom.

The lesson for us is that on the days the lions of the enemy roar around us, the angels of the Lord are standing guard.

PRAYER: *Dear Lord, may we trust you with each crisis that comes into our lives. We thank you for the protection of your love and care that sustains us in our times of greatest need.*

THOUGHT FOR THE DAY: Courage is fear that has said its prayers (author unknown).

# FALLING FOR
# EACH OTHER

## NORMA JEAN MEREDITH WALCHER

*Trust in the LORD with all your heart and lean not on your
own understanding; in all your ways acknowledge him,
and he will make your paths straight.*
—Proverbs 3:5-6

The first time I met M. A. Walcher, he practically fell at my feet. The last hymn had been sung, and the choir was returning to their pews. I was seated on the piano bench playing an old familiar hymn as they filed by. After stumbling, he quickly regained his balance and went to take a seat with his family near the front of the church.

After the service he came to me and asked, "What did you think when I tripped and nearly fell down?" I jokingly replied, "Why, I thought you were falling for me!" We had a big laugh with our spouses gathered around us.

My late husband, Dwight, and I were holding one of our revival services in that little church in Oklahoma back in the 1950s. For more than fifty years he and I traveled as song evangelists, ministering in all forty-eight contiguous states as well as in Canada. Needless to say, I never once again thought about that incident. That is, until a few years ago when I had a friendly reminder.

Although I was officially retired, I kept active singing, playing the piano, and occasionally speaking in nearby churches. After Dwight's death, I continued driving the fifty miles one-way to the church where I was a member when I wasn't scheduled to be someplace else.

However, it wasn't long before that became just too far for this almost-eighty-year-old lady. So I decided to begin attending the church just a few miles south of where I lived. They were very kind and gracious to me.

A new young family moved into that area and began attending the church. One Sunday the young man brought his grandfather to church with his family. He had come to help with work on their ranch.

I was surprised one Sunday following the service when I was talking with someone after the service and felt a tug on my jacket. As I turned, I looked into the face of an older man who smiled and asked, "Do you remember me?"

I replied, "No, sir— don't believe I do."

Then he told me about the time he stumbled as he passed by the piano. He reminded me, "You told me you thought I was falling for you."

It all came back in a flash. I said, "I do remember." And we laughed together.

His family invited me to join them at Pizza Hut after the service. We sat together and talked about the many pastors and evangelists we both knew. He had served as the superintendent of his Sunday School in his church for more than forty years. His wife had passed away six years earlier. Dwight had been gone ten years.

Over the next weeks and months he came to help his grandson often, and I found myself looking forward to his visits. I was disappointed when he didn't come. I found myself reserving a place for him to sit by me in church.

Our relationship developed over the next year and a half. We discovered we had many of the same interests—sports, food, music—and were members of the same denomination. He is kind, gentle, polite, has great integrity, and is deeply committed to the Lord. It wasn't long before I was falling for him!

The day came when we started making plans to get married. Finally I said, "Well, I've not heard four words I need to hear." A blank expression crossed his dear face. I continued, "I'll give you a clue. The first word is "will." He quickly recovered and dropped to one knee right there in the kitchen and asked, "Will you marry me?" I eagerly replied, "In a heartbeat!"

We had a beautiful, simple wedding in the church where we had met fifty years before. God's presence was there as well as dear friends and loved ones. His grandson was best man, and my son was the "man of honor."

We are fully convinced God brought it all together in His timing. When we share our story with anyone who will listen, they agree.

God is our miraculous matchmaker, and in these golden years we're having the times of our lives!

PRAYER: *Thank you, Father, for orchestrating our steps.*

THOUGHT FOR THE DAY: As He guides us, even when we falter, it's clear to see that God has a great sense of humor.

The joy of Jesus is a miracle; it is not
the outcome of my doing things or of
my being good but of my receiving
the very nature of God
(Oswald Chambers,
*My Utmost for His Highest*).

———•———

# MUSTARD SEED FAITH

## LORI WALSH

*If you have faith as small as a mustard seed, you can say to this mountain,
"Move from here to there" and it will move.
Nothing will be impossible for you.*
—Matthew 17:20

An overwhelming cloak of despair fell over me during the spring of
my senior year in college. Following the difficult end of a relationship, I found myself sinking into deep depression. I believe now that
it was not the motivating event that was significant, since pain is
pain, and no one can dictate what should or shouldn't devastate.
Rather, it was my inability to pull myself out of that pit.

I had always possessed a cheerful, glass-half-full personality, and
it shook me to feel so dark and hopeless for weeks and months. I
told very few people that I was struggling and simply cried, read,
and labored through most of that time alone. I sought Christian
counseling, memorized encouraging Bible verses, and made myself
carry on to the best of my ability. Yet I wondered if I could make it
through graduation.

A friend saw my plight and stepped into the gap. Sitting outside one day at a picnic table on the Christian college campus we
attended, Cindy asked if I would fast with her and pray for God to
heal my heart and bring me out of my emotional pit. I reluctantly
agreed, though I felt no hope. I had fasted with my family in previous years—sometimes on Good Friday as a remembrance of Jesus'
sacrifice for me. But I had never fasted in order to bend the ear of
God in my direction. That was new territory for me.

On the day of our planned fast, I numbly walked through the
day, barely noticing the lack of food, since I had no appetite anyway.

As the day passed, though, words to a favorite Christian song of encouragement to trust God's power and ask Him to make a way kept running through my mind.

I pleaded silently with God to simply make a way out for me, though my faith was small.

Late in the afternoon that day, I met Cindy at the prearranged time in the prayer chapel. She must have brought her Bible with her, though the details are blurred now. I remember her reading and praying aloud as we sat close together on a pew in that small, quiet room. My heart was so heavy.

Then something happened. As Cindy continued reading and imploring God to intervene on my behalf, I began sweating, and my heart beat faster. Something like a weight began pressing down on me, and I tried sitting up straighter, feeling a sense of panic rising in me.

Cindy prayed all the more fervently for God's Spirit to overcome whatever was holding me, and I felt a sudden urge to throw up, a vision of the chapel carpet flashing through my mind. Even in that moment, I was horrified that I might ruin the carpet. Then, in an *instant*, it was as though the burden of heaviness lifted and rushed upward and out of me. I stood to my feet, stunned. I was free!

I've always known that God walks with us through the darkest days. I just didn't really expect Him to do that in *my* life. But He did! I know that people of great faith suffer bouts of depression and that God does not always bring instant healing. I simply tell my story as a testimony of God's power to do seemingly impossible things. With Him *anything* is possible.

PRAYER: *Lord, give me faith today to believe that you can perform miracles in my life. Help me to trust you to work in the difficult situations I'm experiencing. I know you love me, and I place myself in your care.*

THOUGHT FOR THE DAY: No pit is so deep that God's love is not deeper still (Corrie ten Boom).

# FREED 52 TO SERVE

## TIM WILKINS

*Tell them how much the Lord has done for you*
*and how he has had mercy on you.*
—Mark 5:19

"Up on your feet so I can knock you down again!" I stood horrified in the middle of our circular hallway as my father shouted those words at my mother, who lay at his feet. Once again, he had knocked her to the living room floor. The fight had awakened me in the middle of the night.

This is one of my earliest childhood memories. I believe I unconsciously made a promise that moment that *I will not be like that man!* I believe that was the beginning of my rejection of masculinity and my ultimate embrace of homosexuality.

Chaos characterized the place we called home. Routinely, tables were overturned, and traumatizing profanity echoed throughout the house. It was not uncommon to find shards of glass covering the floors many mornings from the night before. On one occasion, Dad struck the side of my mother's head with a shoe and burst her eardrum. She cried out in horrible pain. The next night he vowed to do the same thing to the other ear if she did not stop crying.

It that unsettled atmosphere I began sleepwalking. My mother and a brother said I walked to the hallway, knelt facing my parents' bedroom, clasped my throat, and made choking sounds. Although my nightly routine horrified my mother, my father slept through my unconscious cries for help. Neither parent recognized that their youngest son might need counseling.

I remember a summer afternoon when I played alone on a hill beside my house. I longed for a man to model love and protection—

a God-given human need that had gone unmet during my earlier childhood years. I knew I was different even then; something did not fit.

I rarely experienced my father's approval and love. My mother, whose own needs were unmet, turned to me for counsel and help. I became her surrogate husband. She openly expressed to me her disdain for my dad and disgust for sex. She frequently berated me in order to get me to mediate between them.

I was extremely self-conscious and excessively modest. I had never felt I belonged, and my self-esteem was pitifully low. On reaching puberty, I recognized an attraction for guys at school. I did not consciously choose to be attracted to the same sex. One of life's mysteries is that we don't get to choose what tempts us. But I did consciously choose to succumb eventually to those temptations.

When my parents' ballistic tirades reached an intolerable level, Dad left us and went to his parents' house for several months. Once when Dad stopped by for a brief visit, Mama hit him in the back with a flowerpot.

Life at home was hell. Mama manipulated me to get at Dad. When I did not cooperate with her wishes, she accused me, saying, "You love him more than me, don't you?" I didn't want to choose between them; I simply wanted them to love each other and stop fighting.

It was about that time that I gave in to my same-sex attraction to a guy from school who had been my friend for years. His pleasant, approving smile fascinated me. For the first time in my life another male liked me. Thus began my sporadic involvement in homosexual activity. I quickly found that homosexuality provided excitement— but not fulfillment. It gratified but never satisfied.

This activity continued until my early twenties, when I decided that, although I honestly didn't know how not to be homosexual, I did know how to be obedient. I asked God for forgiveness. Then I asked Him to teach me the right way to relate to other men.

When I was twenty-two, I responded to God's call to ministry and went back to college. Living in a men's dorm had a healing effect on me. I was forced to interact with other guys on a daily basis and to learn appropriate relationships.

During the summer months when I was in college, I served as a music and preaching evangelist and youth director. I went from being a shy, introverted, self-conscious wallflower to an assertive man unashamedly proclaiming my love for Christ.

After college I went to Southwestern Seminary. The Bible came alive to me; not only was I receiving a great theological education for a future ministry, but I was also applying biblical truth to my sexual brokenness.

Although same-sex attractions continued throughout college and seminary, I remained steadfast. In fact, by that time I had told God that it didn't matter if I was never attracted to a woman as long as I had Him. That prayer was a milestone. What mattered was being a follower of Jesus Christ.

After graduation I was called to a pastorate in my hometown. My parents had divorced, and Dad had remarried. During this time he went through a foreclosure on his home, a separation from his second wife, alcoholism, and thoughts of suicide. With all the responsibilities of a young, single pastor weighing on my shoulders, I took my father into the parsonage and tended to him until I could enter him into an alcohol abuse facility.

I eventually resigned from that pastorate, disillusioned and depressed. I cried out to God, *What do you want me to do? I've lived a life of celibacy for more than ten years now. I've followed you as closely as I know how. What do you want from me?*

I was about to find out. A good friend from seminary visited my city. I had liked her but never pursued her. We spent several days together. We were affectionate, nothing else, but that was enough. For the first time in my thirty-three years, I experienced a romantic attraction for the opposite sex.

Five years later, I met Lisa at a singles' event, and sparks flew. She was everything I longed for, a beautiful, godly lady with a smile from heaven.

Before we were engaged, I sat down with her for a long talk. "Lisa" I said, "you need to know something about my past, since it may influence our future: I used to be gay." She never wavered in her love for me. We were married August 21, 1993.

More than a year later, Lisa and I were convinced I should go public and share my testimony. I have joyfully proclaimed God's miraculous deliverance to thousands across the country and around the world.

God has blessed Lisa and me enormously. He has given us three precious miracles—our daughters, Clare, Grace, and Ellie. They are the joy of our lives.

I thank the Lord every day for His deliverance. What a blessing to be free from sin's bondage and to share my testimony of God's love and mercy! Truly I have been freed to serve!

PRAYER: *Thank you, Father, for your deliverance.*

THOUGHT FOR THE DAY: We experience true freedom when we embrace Christ as our Deliverer, Lord, and Savior.

# NEVER ALONE

## GAIL BUCHANAN

*Have I not commanded you? Do not be terrified;*
*do not be discouraged, for the LORD your God*
*will be with you wherever you go.*
—Joshua 1:9

Late one evening I was driving home on a dark, lightly traveled road. The inky blackness of that night matched my emotional state. There was so much going wrong in my life. I knew God was in control, but I needed to feel His presence. I prayed softly, asking the Lord to let me know that He still cared about me.

I had taken the shortcut on that narrow two-lane road to get home more quickly. As I drove, waves of uncertainty and concern kept flooding my thoughts and loneliness swept over me.

Suddenly I noticed bright red taillights just ahead. I immediately took my foot off the accelerator, but it wasn't until I was just a few feet from the car ahead of me that I realized it wasn't moving. The driver had stopped to talk with someone driving a car in the opposite direction. The two cars blocked the entire road.

I slammed on my brakes, but I knew it was too late. Gripping the steering wheel with both hands, I practically stood on the brakes. The thoughts of imminent disaster raced through my mind as I slid toward certain injury or death.

My heart cried out to the Lord, asking Him to rescue me and the people in the other cars, as I hit the brakes. I imagined broken bodies and mangled wreckage, and for those few seconds it was as life moved in slow motion.

When my car was practically on top of the car in front of me, it jerked to a screeching stop. The motor stalled out. I was no more than an inch from the other vehicle.

How had I stopped so abruptly? I looked down at the handle that engages the emergency brake, and it was standing straight up! In my panic and fear I hadn't thought to pull it. I remembered my prayer just seconds before, asking the Lord to help me. Had He intervened in this miraculous way?

The car that was heading in the opposite direction peeled off. I was afraid my own car wouldn't start, but when I turned the key in the ignition, it started right up.

I looked in my rearview mirror as I drove away, and I was filled with thanksgiving. Although I had felt alone on that isolated road, my God was with me. The almost tangible presence of the Good Shepherd surrounded me.

For the rest of the drive home I sang songs of praise. I realized that although I had felt alone and forsaken, the Lord was with me all the time. Even when I didn't feel His presence, He had been right beside me.

I was reminded of Joshua 1:9, the scripture my grandmother had shared with me when I was just six years old. She promised me that God would always be with me.

He is always with us. We are never alone.

PRAYER: *Thank you, Heavenly Father, for surrounding us with your precious, protecting presence in life's darkest moments.*

THOUGHT FOR THE DAY: If we abide in Jesus, He carries us through the storms of life.

# CONCLUSION

As we've journeyed together through these accounts of encounters with God from around the world, I pray that your faith walk has been strengthened. May we renew our determination to travel onward through the unknown trails of life, venturing forth into each moment with strong faith in our Heavenly Father. We can rest assured that those of us whose hope is firmly anchored to Him will always be sustained. We can depend upon our Lord to lead, guide, and guard us in all circumstances.

Trusting our tomorrows to the one who has already been there enables us to have peace regardless of what new crisis may arise. May we always remember that life's calamities are stage settings for divine appointments with the ultimate miracle-worker. So as we keep our eyes firmly fixed on Him, we can expect more "God sightings" in the days that lie ahead.

# ABOUT THE CONTRIBUTORS

**Judy Anderson** is a popular speaker, Bible study teacher, and musician. She and her husband, Daryl, live in Wichita, Kansas.

**David Argabright** is CEO of Argabright Contractors. He has coordinated more than 100 Work and Witness teams since 1982. He and his family share the gospel around the world. He and his wife, Sharon, live in Vinton, Virginia.

**Larry Belew** is an ordained minister who ministers to developmentally challenged adults. He also teaches music in a public school. He and his wife, Judie, live in Wichita, Kansas.

**Jane Berry** is a hair stylist and serves as women's ministries director at her local church. She and her husband, Danny, live in Oklahoma City.

**Jill Briscoe** has worked with her husband in ministry for more than forty years. She is a prolific writer and in demand as a keynote speaker for Christian events. She and her husband, Stuart, live in Milwaukee.

**Gail Buchanan** is a musician who has sung with many groups including the Singing Quakers. She and her husband, Tim, have two children and live in Andover, Kansas.

**Gracia Burnham** is a popular speaker and the author of the award-winning book *In the Presence of My Enemies*. She lives with her children in Rose Hill, Kansas.

**Paul Burnham** is a member of New Tribes Mission. He and his wife, Oreta, served thirty-four years in the Philippines in church planting and Bible translation. They live in Rose Hill, Kansas.

**Patti Cappa** is a marriage and family therapist. She is executive director of Marble Retreat in the Colorado Rockies, where she teams with her psychologist husband, Steve. They live in Marble, Colorado.

**Tina Coggins** is a motivational speaker and inspirational singer. She and her husband, Ken, live in Newnan, Georgia.

**Sandy Combs** is an artist by trade and a Christian by definition. She uses her art to demonstrate the blessings of God in our lives. She and her husband of thirty-eight years live in Key Largo, Florida.

**Tom Cornelius** currently serves on the pastoral staff of Believers Tabernacle in Wichita, Kansas, where he is the director of The Wichita Dream Center. He and his wife, Judy, live in Wichita.

**Carole Costa** is retired from the faculty of Trevecca Nazarene University in Nashville. She has worked on fifteen Work and Witness trips. She and her husband, Roger, live in Hermitage, Tennessee.

**Rachael Crabb** formerly served on the national board of Stonecroft Ministries. She is an author and serves on the advisory board for MOPS (Mothers of Preschoolers). She and her husband, Larry, live in Morrison, Colorado.

**Wayne Crouch** is retired from Norfolk Southern Corporation. He and his wife, Polly Anne, live in Chesterfield, Virginia.

**Jun Detalo** is the district superintendent of the Bicol District of the Church of the Nazarene in the Philippines. He has pastored for thirty years and is also a school principal. He and his wife, Nancy, live in Banadero, Legazpi City, Philippines.

**Solomon Dinakaran** pastors a church in Whitefield, India, where he lives with his wife, Selvi.

**Scott Dooley** is a missionary physician at Nazarene Hospital in Papua New Guinea. He and his wife, Gail, live in Mt. Hagen, Papua New Guinea.

**Beth Ellenberg** is a full-time pastor, and she and her husband, Tim, also conduct marriage enrichment retreats. They live in Lexington, Kentucky.

**Worku Geremew** was born in Addis Ababa, Ethiopia. He is the director and founder of Rise Together Ministries. He earned a master of divinity degree from the Asian Center for Theological Studies and Missions in South Korea. He and his wife, Rebecca, are starting an orphanage in Ethiopia. They live in St. Louis.

**Kendra Graham** is a gifted speaker, a registered nurse, and enjoys running marathons. She and her husband, Wil, live in Swannanoa, North Carolina.

**Nina G. Gunter** is a general superintendent emeritus in the Church of the Nazarene, the first woman to serve as general superintendent in the denomination. She is a preacher, teacher, and author. She and her husband, Moody, live near Nashville.

**Brian Helstrom** is a missionary with the Church of the Nazarene and executive director of *JESUS* Film Harvest Partners. Brian and his wife, Jeanie, live in Olathe, Kansas.

**Phyllis Pennington Hill** is retired from Principal Financial Group. She and her husband have traveled to several countries on Work and Witness trips. Phyllis and her husband, David, live in Wichita, Kansas.

**Aletha Hinthorn** is the founder of Women Alive Ministries, director of Come to the Fire Conferences, and the author of several books. She and her husband, Daniel, live in Leawood, Kansas.

**George H. Hunley II** has served as a minister in the Church of the Nazarene for more than twenty-six years. He is completing his doctorate in Bible and theology. He and his wife, Christie, live in Louisa, Virginia.

**Karen Kingsbury** is a best-selling inspirational Christian fiction author with nearly five million books currently in print. She lives with her husband and children in the Pacific Northwest.

**Randy Ledsome** is a speaker, musician, and pastor who enjoys training and equipping others for ministry. He and his wife, Susan, live in Elkview, West Virginia.

**Lorrie Lindgren** is CEO of Women of the Harvest, a ministry providing support and encouragement to women serving cross-culturally. She and her husband, Jim, live in Lakewood, Colorado.

**Janice Long** works part time in order to be available to her family. She is especially gifted in reaching out to others with the good news of the gospel of Jesus Christ. She and her husband, Miles, live in Olathe, Kansas.

**Paula Martin** is office manager for a family-owned investment firm. She and her husband, Jerry, live in Andover, Kansas.

**Kim McLean** is a gifted songwriter who has won numerous awards. Her transparency in talking about her life and her love for Jesus impacts her listeners. She lives in the Nashville area.

**Holly Miller** is the author of *Life After the Games*. She and her husband, Charles, reside in Wichita, Kansas.

**Beth Moore** is a well-known speaker, author, and Bible teacher and is the founder of Living Proof Ministries. She speaks and teaches across the United States as well as in other countries.

**Larry Page** has served as a student ministries pastor for more than fifteen years, following his lifelong calling and passion. He and his wife, Crystal, live in Wichita, Kansas.

**Gary Parrish** is an emergency room physician who ministers to those who come under his care. He is a native Floridian who divides his time between Florida and Virginia.

**Kim Pound** and her husband, Darin, have recently left the pastorate to go to the mission field. They currently live and minister in Dangriga, Belize, in Central America.

**Brad Riley** is associate pastor of First Church of the Nazarene in Wichita, Kansas, where he lives with his wife, Rhonda.

**Dana Roberts** is a stay-at-home mom who uses her training as a teacher to teach the Bible, to mentor, and to volunteer in her community. She and her husband, Kevin, live in Spring, Texas.

**Kim Singson** is district superintendent on the North East India District of the Church of the Nazarene. She has helped plant many churches in her district and is a *JESUS* film coach. A widow, Kim lives with her children in Churachandpur, India.

**Rick Underwood** is senior stewardship officer at Trevecca Nazarene University as well as a licensed professional counselor and director of the counseling ministry at his church. Rick and his wife, Donna, live in Nashville.

**Kelly Jo Vanderstelt** home schools her daughter and is involved in worship and women's ministries at North Bay Community Church, where her husband serves as pastor. She and her husband, Curt, live in Superior, Wisconsin.

**Norma Jean Meredith Walcher** traveled for many years with her first husband, Dwight, as they served as song evangelists across the United States. After his death, Norma Jean continued her ministry through music. She and her husband, M. A. Walcher, live in Choctaw, Oklahoma.

**Lori Walsh** and her husband, Chris, have served in numerous ministry capacities. She is a substitute teacher and serves alongside her husband, who is executive pastor at First Mennonite Brethren Church. They live in Wichita, Kansas.

**Tim Wilkins** shares his deliverance from homosexuality through his ministry, Cross Ministry. He and his wife, Lisa, live in Wake Forest, North Carolina.